AF600410

THE CATHOLIC UNIVERSITY OF AMERICA
CANON LAW STUDIES
No. 327

ENTRANCE INTO THE NOVITIATE BY CLERICS IN MAJOR ORDERS

A HISTORICAL SYNOPSIS AND A COMMENTARY

A DISSERTATION
Submitted to the Faculty of the School of Canon Law
of the Catholic University of America
in Partial Fulfillment
of the Requirements for the Degree
of Doctor of Canon Law

by

THE REVEREND LEO KOESLER, O.S.B., J.C.L.
New Subiaco Abbey
Subiaco, Arkansas

THE CATHOLIC UNIVERSITY OF AMERICA
WASHINGTON, D. C.
1953

IMPRIMI POTEST:

✠ PAULUS M. NAHLEN, O.S.B., Abbas Monasterii Neo-Sublacensis.
Die 29 iunii, 1951.

NIHIL OBSTAT:

HIERONYMUS D. HANNAN, A.M., LL.B., S.T.D., J.C.D.,
Censor Deputatus.

IMRIMATUR:

✠ PATRICIUS A. O'BOYLE, D.D., Archiepiscopus Washingtonensis.
Washingtonii, die 9 iunii, 1951.

Printed by The Abbey Press, St. Meinrad, Indiana

IN HONOR OF
THE IMMACULATE HEART OF MARY

TABLE OF CONTENTS

Part Two

CANONICAL COMMENTARY

CHAPTER VI

CHAPTER VII

CHAPTER VIII

FOREWORD

The title of this dissertation is: "Entrance into the Novitiate by Clerics in Major Orders." It treats of the first listed impediment against licit admission into the novitiate. In the Code of Canon Law there are mentioned six impediments under the rather general division of canon 542, 2°. In order to distinguish this single impediment in referring to canon 542, 2°, from the remaining five, especially when possible confusion may result from the lack of such distinction, it is deemed advisable to qualify the number (2°) with the abbreviated form (*pr.*) of the word, *primus*, which designation of the impediment will be written thus, canon 542, 2° *pr.* Any other impediment or requisite for a cleric's entrance into religion is considered only in so far as this is necessary to delineate the extent of the local ordinary's canonical right to object to the cleric's permanent departure from the diocese and of the cleric's liberty to embrace the religious life.

The actual reason for the transfer of a secular, major cleric to the religious life will not be considered. No comparisons will be drawn between the religious state and the clerical state, or between the perfections of the two states. The objective transfer of a major cleric from the service of the diocese to membership in a religious institute forms the basic background of this study. On account of the very nature of the impediment of canon 542, 2° *pr.*, it is necessary to refer frequently to a cleric's departure from his diocese in order to enter a novitiate, and thereby it is possible to create a false opinion that the priesthood as such is more sublime in a religious than in a diocesan priest. But it is a well known and accepted truth that the sacred orders of subdiaconate, diaconate, and priesthood are of the same sublime excellence, whether they have been bestowed upon a religious or a secular cleric.

In Part One, the historical synopsis indicates the complete and unrestricted freedom of clerics in early times to leave the service of their church in order to enter a religious community. In the thirteenth century is found the development of a restriction upon this liberty by the fact that a local ordinary was allowed to recall his former clerical subject to the service of the abandoned church, if serious harm resulted to that church.

Part Two introduced the present legislation, by which a formal impediment against licit entrance into the novitiate is directed against a major, but not a minor, cleric in two instances: 1) when he seeks admission without previously consulting his local ordinary; 2) when he leaves the service of the diocese in opposition to the local ordinary's judgment a) that grave harm will result to souls upon the cleric's departure, and b) that this injury cannot at all be averted by means of other arrangements.

In the canonical commentary, which is composed of Part Two, there are three chapters which specify the clerics affected by this impediment and those not so influenced, the meaning of consultation with the local ordinary, and finally the one and only justified opposition to the major cleric's transfer to religion on the part of the local ordinary.

The present writer wishes to express his sincere gratitude to his Abbot, the Right Reverend Paul Nahlen, O.S.B., and the community of New Subiaco Abbey for the opportunity of advanced study in Canon Law, to the members of the Faculty of the School of Canon Law for their scholarly direction and valuable assistance, and to all others who by their kind encouragement and earnest prayers contributed towards the completion of this dissertation.

PART ONE

HISTORICAL SYNOPSIS

CHAPTER I

HISTORICAL DEVELOPMENT BEFORE THE TIME OF GRATIAN

ARTICLE 1. MONASTIC LEGISLATION

In the early monastic Rules where reference is made to the admission of clerics to the monastery, legislation of a rather general nature only can be found.

St. Pachomius († 345), in his Rule for eastern monasticism, refers to clerics entering the monastery, how they are to be received and what hospitality should be shown them.[1]

However, in the Rule attributed to certain Fathers of the fourth century, a distinction was made in the manner of receiving clerics. Seemingly, only lapsed clerics, repentant of their past sins, were granted permission to enter the monastery.[2]

St. Benedict (480-547), Father of Western Monasticism, legislated in his Rule for the reception of priests and clerics into the monastery. If any of them sought admission, it was not to be granted them too hastily, nor was anything to be relaxed in their favor.[3]

In commenting on the sixtieth chapter of the Rule of St. Benedict wherein this subject is treated, St. Benedict of Aniane († 821) stated that the cloisters of the monks

[1] Cap. 15, *Regula Sancti Pachomii*—Migne, *Patrologiae Cursus Completus, Series Latina* (221 vols., Parisiis, 1844-1864), XXIII, 70 (hereafter cited as *MPL*).

[2] Cap. 14, *Regula Sanctorum Serapionis, Macarii, Paphnutii et alterius Macarii*—*Codex Regularum Monasticarum et Canonicarum*, collected by St. Benedict of Aniane (6 vols., Augustae Vindelicorum, 1759), I.

[3] Cap. 60, *Sancti Benedicti Regula Monachorum*, ed. by C. Butler (Friburgi-Brisgoviae, 1912); cf. Sister M. Alfred Schroll, O.S.B., *Benedictine Monasticism* (New York: Columbia University Press, 1941), p. 73; Delatte, *A Commentary on the Rule of St. Benedict* (New York: Benziger Brothers, 1921), p. 314.

were always open to clerics desirous of penance and a higher life. And this pertained not only to lapsed clerics, for by the authority of the abbot the candidates would be permitted to retain their office of blessing and of saying Mass. This the legislator would not have allowed so readily to any clerics of reprobate character. Since Pope Gregory (590-604) approved this Rule of St. Benedict, he also authorized the practice of receiving priests and clerics into the Order.[4] It is to be noted that no mention is made as to whether or not these clerics had consulted their bishop, or asked his leave before embracing the monastic state. Yet, when St. Benedict directed how monks from other monasteries were to be received, he was quite explicit in demanding that no abbot accept into his community a monk from any known monastery without the consent of his abbot and without letters of recommendation, because it is written: 'See thou never do to another what thou wouldst hate to have done to thee by another.'[5] Likewise no evidence is to be found in the others Rules cited above that consultation of his bishop was demanded of a cleric entering religion.

ARTICLE 2. COUNCILS AND CAPITULARIES

From the legislation of several councils, it is likewise evident that the admission of priests and clerics into the monastery was not exceptional. No special requisites other than those demanded in a lay candidates were required.

At the Council of Saragossa (380) held in Spain, an enactment was passed concerning their admission. Clerics were not to seek admission for vanity's sake, that they might seem to be more observant of the law than other clerics. Neither was the monastery to accept such clerical applicants unless during a time of probation they had proved themselves to be of the right spirit and intention. This canon

[4] *Concordia Regularum*—MPL, CIII, 1313.
[5] *Loc. cit.*

was instituted in opposition to the false sanctity of the heretic Priscillianus and his followers.[6]

In the year 633, the IV Council of Toledo determined that bishops ought (*oportet*) not to prevent their clerics from entering the monastery if these subjects wanted to do this in order to lead a better and holier life (*meliorem vitam*).[7]

Again, in 653, the VIII Council of Toledo legislated that those clerics who had received the monastic habit were obliged to be true clerics and monks. Otherwise they were to be corrected.[8]

The mild legislation of the IV Council of Toledo was repeated, but in stronger terms, by a Synod of Augsburg in 952. In no way was the entrance of clerics into the monastery to be prevented. On the contrary, they were to be encouraged to persevere in their choice of a stricter life.[9]

The first mention of any necessary permission from the bishop to join the religious life is found in Charlemagne's Capitulary (789). He forbade strange and fugitive clerics to be received or ordained without commendatory letters and the permission of their bishop.[10]

Another Monastic Capitulary (817) declared that only

[6] C. 6—H. Th. Bruns, *Canones Apostolorum et Conciliorum Saeculorum IV, V, VI, VII* (2 vols., Berolini, 1839), II, 14 (hereafter cited as Bruns); cf. Notes on this council in Mansi, *Sacrorum Conciliorum Nova et Amplissima Collection* (53 vols. in 59, Paris-Arnhem-Leipzig, 1901-1927), III, 640 (hereafter cited as Mansi).

[7] Cap. un., C. XIX, q. 1—*Corpus Iuris Canonici* (2. ed., curavit Friedberg, 2 vols., Lipsiae, 1879-1881) (hereafter all citations from the *Corpus Iuris Canonici* will be made from this edition); Bruns, I, 235.

[8] C. 3, X, *de regularibus et transeuntibus ad religionem*, III, 31.

[9] Cap. 7: "Clericis monachicum habitum sequi cupientibus et pro remuneratione divina saecularibus spretis arctiorem vitam adire volentibus, nullatenus introeundi aditus ab episcopo denegetur, sed potius eum in tali conversatione perstare exhortari conetur. . ."—Mansi, XVIII, 438.

[10] *Monumenta Germaniae Historica, Legum Sectio II, Capitularia Regum Francorum*, tom. I (ed. A. Boretius, Hannoverae: 1883), n. 3.

those secular priests and clerics who intended to become monks were allowed residence in the monastery.[11]

Article 3. Private Responses Not Found in the Decree of Gratian and the Decretals of Gregory IX

The writings of popes and of an archbishop, besides restating at least indirectly the right of clerics to join the religious life, emphasized that a) a cleric who had been accepted into a monastery could not freely return to his former church or office; b) a cleric could not of his own accord transfer from one church to another in his diocese without the consent of his bishop.

In regard to the first point, there was a letter of Pope Gregory the Great to a certain subdeacon, Anthemius. If for any reason, the Pope said, a cleric should transfer to the monastic life, he was not to return of his own accord to his former or any other church.[12]

There can be no doubt that a cleric who wanted to transfer from one church to another, or simply desired to relinquish the one under his charge, needed the permission of his bishop. An instance of this was indicated in a private reply when Pope Gregory's opinion was asked concerning the fitness for the episcopacy of a certain Archdeacon John who might be elected. He answered that no one appeared to be so worthy for the position as John the Archdeacon. Yet, should he be elected, his own bishop would first "have to give him leave to go, that he may be found free to be ordained."[13]

In the two following letters a new development in the subject under discussion was brought into consideration. A deacon, Pancratius, who had chosen the monastic state, was recalled by his bishop, Desiderius, of the Diocese of Vienne in southern Gaul. To know the mind of the Church

[11] *Ibid.*, n. 42.

[12] Lib. I, ep. 40—Mansi, IX, 1058; cf. lib. IV, ep. 1—Mansi, IX, 1186; lib. IV, ep. 18—Mansi, IX, 1197.

[13] Lib. V, ep. 17—*Nicene and Post Nicene Fathers*, Vol. XII (2. series, New York: Parker and Company, 1895), p. 165.

in so delicate a matter, the deacon explained the entire happenings to Pope Gregory, also mentioning that he had been attached to a cleric's office in his bishop's church before entering the monastery. But then, moved by divine inspiration, he sought the favor of a monastic vocation and consequently was admitted. To clear up this troublesome situation, Pope Gregory wrote to the bishop who had recalled the deacon and urged him not to impede this cleric in his purpose, but rather zealously to encourage him to fulfill what he had begun.[14]

That Pope Gregory would not allow the aforesaid archdeacon to leave the service of his church without his bishop's permission, but in the case just described permitted the deacon to remain in the monastery, is of some importance in this work.[15]

Anselm, Archbishop of Canterbury († 1109), furnished us with a similar case. A *cantor* of Paris had joined the monastery of St. Martin. This choice of a higher vocation gave joy to the archbishop, though later he was saddened upon hearing that the *cantor* was recalled by his bishop. The archbishop feared that the devil was deceiving the cleric, causing him to think that he was doing the correct thing since the bishop had recalled him. But the *cantor* was not to acquiesce to this false notion. To return would indeed cause reproof from the evil spirit who defended his argumentation in the bishop's revocation. Yet "no one putting his hand to the plough and looking back is fit for the kingdom of God."[16] But he was looking back from Christ's plough if he desisted to follow the vocation he had begun to pursue. Furthermore, just as bishops preserve their authority when agreeing with Christ, so they

[14] Lib. X, ep. 39—Mansi, X, 332.

[15] Cf. Benedictus XIV, ep. *Ex quo dilectus,* 14 ian. 1747—*Codicis Iuris Canonici Fontes,* cura Emi Petri Card. Gasparri editi (9 vols., Romae [postea Civitate Vaticana]: Typis Polyglottis Vaticanis, 1923-1939 [vols. VII, VIII, IX, ed. cura et studio Emi Iustiniani Card. Seredi]), II, 374 (hereafter cited as *Fontes*).

[16] Luke, IX, 62.

lose it (*sibi eam adimunt*) when disagreeing with Him.[17] Only in the former case are the faithful expected to follow him. After some further similar instruction and exhortation, Anselm concluded that the *cantor* could have begun nothing more salutary and could relinquish nothing with greater danger. Therefore he should not allow anything to prevent him from returning to the monastic life. And finally he should read the legislation of the IV Council of Toledo (633), which treats of clerics desirous of embracing the monastic life.[18]

This narrative provides a second instance, therefore, in which it was contended that a cleric who had entered the monastic life was not to be recalled. Yet, the fact that the respective bishops had done so, apparently without malice or evil intent, shows that no explicit legislation had been enacted in this regard. It might also be remarked that no mention was made as to whether the deacon Pancratius and the *cantor* had, prior to entering religion, consulted their respective ecclesiastical superiors or had obtained their permission. It seems that they had done neither. Otherwise they could hardly have been expected to return.

Pope Pascal II (1099-1118), in writing to a certain John, Prior of the Church of St. Peter de Valeriis, opened his letter by proclaiming his solicitude for the welfare of the entire Church, especially of the subjects immediately under the jurisdiction of the Holy See. Hence he stated that he wished, with the help of God, to provide sufficiently for them. Therefore he directed that no bishop or prelate should prevent monks from receiving lay and secular clerics into their ranks.[19]

[17] Whether this was correct canonically can readily be questioned.

[18] Lib. III, ep. 13—*MPL*, CLIX, 37-38; cf. lib. II, ep. 12—*MPL*, CLVIII, 1160-1165.

[19] Ep. 400—*MPL*, CLXIII, 360; Jaffé, *Regesta Pontificum Romanorum a condita Ecclesia ad annum post Christum natum MCXCVIII* (2. ed. by F. Kaltenbrunner [ad annum 590], Ewald [590-882], and S. Loewenfeld [882-1198], and so referred to as: JK, JE and JL, 2 vols., Lipsiae, 1885-1888), JL, n. 6413.

The aforementioned letters have not been included in the Decree of Gratian (1140) or in the Decretals of Gregory IX (1234). Others of similar import, however, were mentioned in these collections of church legislation and will be discussed in the following chapter.

CHAPTER II

FROM THE DECREE OF GRATIAN TO THE COUNCIL OF TRENT

Article 1. The Decree of Gratian

In the nineteenth cause of the second book, Gratian († 1157) treated *ex professo*, though briefly, the legislation affecting clerics entering a monastery.[1]

In his *causa* Gratian presented the problem. A cleric had asked his bishop's permission to transfer to the monastic state. But this the bishop was unwilling to grant. In spite of the refusal, the cleric abandoned his church and joined the monastic family. With this in mind Gratian proposed two questions: a) Is a bishop bound to grant his permission to a cleric so that, renouncing his proper church, the cleric may enter a monastery? b) May a cleric join a monastery if his bishop, unwilling to let him go, refuses permission?[2]

As regards the first, Gratian answered that the bishop was obliged to give (*dare debeat*) his permission. In confirmation of this response he quoted from the IV Council of Toledo (633) that a cleric who sought the monastic life was to be allowed by his bishop to follow his objective because he desired a higher life. He was not to be hindered in any way.[3]

In regard to the second question, Gratian answered that a cleric should not be received by any one if the bishop has denied him leave.[4] Yet this norm does not control, he immediately added, if the cleric should desire to advance to a higher life. For in the latter case he would be free to go, although his bishop objected.[5]

[1] Cf. C. XIX, qq. 1 and 2.

[2] Pr., C. XIX.

[3] C. un., C. XIX, q. 1; Bruns, I, 235.

[4] C. 1, C. XIX, q. 2; taken from a letter of Pope Leo (440-461) to Bishop Anastasius of Thessalonica, a. 446(?)—JE, n. 411.

[5] Dictum p. c. 1, C. XIX, q. 2.

In support of this contention he quoted a letter of Pope Urban II (1088-1999) to the monastery of St. Rufinus. Its chapter had asked the Pope what the law was concerning secular clerics who wished to enter a monastery while their bishop was opposed to such transfer of his clerics. To this the Pontiff replied that two kinds of laws had to be considered: one public and another private. The public law, confirmed by the writings of the saintly Fathers, was enacted on account of transgressions. For example, it was decreed in the canons that a cleric was not allowed to transfer from one church to another, without commendatory letters from his bishop. This must be so because it had happened that an unworthy cleric, not allowed to exercise his functions in one diocese, simply decided to perform them in another diocese. But the private law was from the inspiration of the Holy Spirit. This law was written in the heart of man, as says the Apostle: "They have the law of God written in their hearts." And if any secular cleric entrusted with the care of souls should be led by the private law to save himself in some monastery, he should not by a public law be restrained from following his desire. Of greater dignity was the private law than the public. Whoever, therefore, was led by the Holy Spirit, even though the bishop opposed him, was considered free to enter the religious life. This he would do by authority of the Pope.[6]

The *glossa ordinaria* raised several objections: how could a cleric who was bound to his bishop by an oath leave the diocese of the latter and pass over to a monastery,

[6] C. 2, C. XIX, q. 2; JE, n. 5760; Mansi, XX, 714; *MPL*, CLI, 535. In the footnote to this canon, Friedberg placed a question mark in parentheses after the name of Urban II, thereby indicating the doubtful authenticity of the canon. Yet the possibility that the letter is not Urban II's does not destroy its value in this present work, for Pope Benedict XIV referred to the same canon to confirm his position, admitted the distinction between the public and private law, and quoted at length from the same letter. Cf. Claeys Bouuaert, *De Canonica Cleri Saecularis obedientia* (Lovanii, 1904), p. 196.

when his bishop was unwilling to grant him leave? Furthermore, not to obey was idolatry. Oftentimes even good had to be omitted on account of the merit of obedience. Finally, a cleric was forbidden to alienate ecclesiastical goods. How much less could he alienate his own person who was of greater worth than property? The *glossa* unraveled these difficulties by a very short and simple solution: the cleric was still free to leave for the monastery because he acted according to the inspiration of the Holy Spirit.[7]

The Decretists had little to add concerning this legisaltion. Rufinus († 1190),[8] Huguccio († 1210)[9] and Guido de Bayso († 1313)[10] agreed on the general principle that a cleric had the right to enter the monastic life, although his bishop refused permission. Joannes Teutonicus († 1245 or 1246) in the context seemed to say that this right was similar to that of a monk or canon regular who, having requested though not received his superior's consent, might transfer to a stricter life.[11] The greater austerity is a sufficient reason.[12] Rufinus, however, remarked that a cleric may do this only for a true, religious purpose, not out of pretence, levity, ambition or for similar reasons.[13]

The *glossa ordinaria* and the Decretists made no distinction as to whether the cleric was in possession of a benefice, or whether the forsaking of it would cause scandal among people or harm to the Church. The letter of Urban II[14]

[7] *Glossa ordinaria* ad c. 2, C. XIX, qu. 2, s. v. *Si afflatus—Decretum Gratiani Emendatum et Observationibus Illustratum una cum Glossis, Gregorii XIII Pont. Max. iussu editum* (2 vols., Romae,, 1582) (hereafter all citations from the *glossa ordinaria* will be taken from this edition).

[8] Ad c. 1, C. XIX, q. 2—*Die Summa Decretorum des Magister Rufinus* (Paderborn, 1902).

[9] *Glossa ordinaria* ad pr., C. XIX, q. 1, s. v. *Quod episcopus.*

[10] N. 1, *Rosarium seu in Decretorum Volumen Commentaria* (Venetiis, 1577), commenting on the rubrics of C. XIX.

[11] *Glossa* pr., C. XIX, q. 1, s. v. *Quod episcopus.*

[12] *Ibid.,* s. v. *meliorem.*

[13] Ad v. *Quod episcopus licentiam—Op. cit.,* c. 1, C. XIX, q. 1.

[14] *Supra,* p. 9.

did explicitly apply it even to the beneficed clergy. So it is only logical to conclude that they were of the same opinion, since they did not distinguish in their commentaries. But the Decretalists in developing the legislation as found in Gregory IX's collection did take into consideration probable resulting scandal and serious loss to the Church.

Article 2. The Decretals of Gregory IX

A. The Transfer of Religious to Another Community

By means of the papal Constitution, *Rex Pacificus,* (September 5, 1234), Pope Gregory IX promulgated the Decretals. This gave to his collection of previous legislation authentic and legal force.[15]

In regard to the matter under discussion, Gregory IX did not treat it directly. He did, however, incorporate the famous letter (dated April 29, 1206) of Innocent III (1198-1216), which allowed the transfer of religious to a holier life.[16]

From this letter and from Gratian's Decree the Decretalists drew the conclusion by analogy that under similar conditions a cleric might also pass over to a religious life. Because of the intimate connection of these important points, it will be necessary to examine more closely its contents.

A monk of Durham (Cathedral monastery) had gone over to the Cistercians. His prior molested him by saying that to leave the monastery (for a stricter life) without permission was not allowed. Pope Innocent III heard of this trouble and explained the matter to the Prior and the community.

[15] Amleto Giovanni Cicognani, *Canon Law* (2. ed., Westminster, Maryland: The Newman Bookshop, copyright 1934), pp. 298-302.

[16] C. 18 (*Licet*), X, *de regularibus et transeuntibus ad religionem,* III, 31; Potthast, *Regesta Pontificum Romanorum inde ab anno post Christum Natum 1198 ad annum 1304* (2 vols., Berolini, 1874-1875), n. 2763 (hereafter cited as Potthast).

Although some monks, canons regular, hospitallers,[17] and templars[18] had received an indult from the Holy See restraining the transfer of any of their professed members to a stricter religious life, this privilege was to be interpreted as a restriction only upon those members who would transfer out of temerity or light-mindedness with a consequent loss or injury to the Order. But, Pope Innocent continued, it did not apply to those members who conceived their desire with humility and purity of heart, for they were led by the Holy Spirit and possessed freedom under the private law. Such were not bound by the public law.[19] Therefore if a religious with motives of this kind had received a negative reply to his petition for a transfer, he was still considered free to fulfill his holy designs, regardless of the indiscreet refusal. This procedure was allowable because he who abused his authority deserved to lose it. Truly a prelate should not deny this to his subject, for just as the latter was bound to request permission lest he seem to disdain holy obedience, so the prelate must consider it his duty readily to grant it.

Yet if a probable doubt existed as to the subject's motives, or the strictness of the other Order, it was necessary to seek the judgment of a higher superior.

Innocent III also mentioned that without the consent of the Pope bishops were never allowed to desert their flock for the sake of a monastic vocation.[20]

In this particular case, the monk who had transferred to the Cistercians was not to be troubled, because he had

[17] The Knights Hospitallers of St. John, a Military Order, were meant. Raymond of Puy drew up their statutes in 1118, which were approved by Pope Innocent II (1130-1143).

[18] A Military Order founded as a society of laymen in 1118.

[19] Innocent III referred to the letter of Urban II.

[20] Since this is outside the scope of the present work, it is of interest only in so far as it furnishes the basis for opinions by Decretalists as to whether an abbot or other prelates of rank inferior to that of bishops are bound by the same restriction. Cf. *infra, pp.* 16, 17.

done so with a pure intention and good conscience.[21] But according to Abbas Panormitanus († ca. 1453) such a religious was to be returned to his former monastery if from the transfer it had suffered serious harm or defamation.[22]

The glosses of the *glossa ordinaria* to this canon were quite similar to those in the Decree of Gratian. Again the objections were raised as to how anyone could alienate his own person when his prelate was opposed to this, if he was not even allowed to alienate ecclesiastical goods without the bishop's consent.[23] Especially it was asked how a cleric could do this when he was bound by an oath to obey his Superior.[24] And oftentimes good was to be omitted for the sake of obedience.[25] Then it answered very briefly and simply that a religious still may transfer under the inspiration of the Holy Spirit; he is not restricted by the public law.[26] In virtue of the private law of God, His love in the heart of man, is this allowed.[27]

[21] Cf. *glossa ordinaria* s. v. *licentiam postulaverit* ad c. 18, X, *de regularibus et transeuntibus ad religionem,* III, 31. Latest research places the date of the final text of the *glossa ordinaria* between the years 1263-1266; cf. S. Kuttner-Beryl Smalley, "The Glossa Ordinaria to the Gregorian Decretals, "*The English Historical Review* (London, 1886—), LX (1945), 97-105.

[22] (Nicolaus de Tudeschis), *Commentaria in Quinque Libros Decretalium* (5 vols. in 7, Venetiis, 1578), lib. III, tit. 31, c. 18, n. 12 (hereafter cited as Panormitanus).

[23] *Loc. cit.* This same objection is advanced by Panormitanus, *loc. cit.*; cf. Hostiensis (Henricus de Segusio), *Commentaria in Quinque Libros Decretalium* (5 vols. in 3, Venetiis, 1581), lib. II, tit. 31, c. 18, n. 12 (hereafter cited as Hostiensis).

[24] *Glossa ordinaria, loc. cit.;* of the same opinion was Hostiensis, *ibid.*, n. 9.

[25] *Glossa ordinaria, loc. cit.;* the same objection is advanced by Hostiensis, lib. III, tit. 31, c. 18, n. 10.

[26] *Glossa ordinaria, loc. cit.*

[27] Laurentius Hispanus, as quoted in the *glossa ordinaria* s. v. *ex lege privata,* ad c. 18, X, *de regularibus et transeuntibus ad religionem,* III, 31.

B. The Admission of Clerics into the Monastic Life

From analogy with this legislation and its interpretation, the Decretalists argued that under similar circumstances a secular cleric had the right to embrace the monastic life. Although a religious was required to seek permission at least for his transfer in order to avoid contempt of authority and sinning against obedience, a cleric was allowed to enter without asking the bishop's permission.[28] But if he had been entrusted with the care of souls, and his church would suffer a serious loss, he could not leave it in this abrupt way. In such a case, if he did leave, his church could demand his return just as it could demand a *restitutio in integrum* should it be injured in a temporal manner.[29] Joannes Andreae († 1348) likewise specified that a beneficed cleric, before renouncing the office to enter religion, was required at least to consult his bishop, although it was not necessary that he should have received his permission. To renounce his office for any other reason, the cleric needed his bishop's consent. If the cleric acted without that consent, he could be punished.[30]

Panormitanus again repeated that if serious harm accrued to the church formerly under the cleric's charge, he could be recalled. This conclusion he based on the statement of Innocent IV (1254) who in his commentary expressed his preference for the opinion that such a cleric could be recalled.[31] He also argued from the parallel legis-

[28] Panormitanus, lib. III, tit. 31, c. 18, nn. 10 and 12. Pope Innocent IV: "... Clericus aut transire ad religionem poterit non petita licentia, etiam petita contradicatur ut c. 2, c. XIX, q. 2. Crederemus tamen, quod posset eum repetere, si ex transitu suo prima ecclesia gravem sustineret iacturam."—*Apparatus super Quinque Libris Decretalium* (Strassburg, 1478), lib. III, tit. 31, c. 18, 14th division (hereafter cited as Innocent IV).

[29] Panormitanus, *ibid.*, n. 12; Hostiensis, *ibid.*, n. 6.

[30] *In Sex Decretalium Libros Novella Commentaria* (6 vols. in 5, Venetiis, 1581), lib. I, tit. 9, c. 4, nn. 8 and 1 (hereafter cited as Joannes Andreae).

[31] Panormitanus, *ibid.*, n. 14. The statement of Innocent IV is found in footnote 28, on this page.

lation of the canon *Admonet* of Pope Alexander III (1159-1181) and from a like canon in the Decree of Gratian. Pope Alexander III had admonished a bishop to forbid his clerics to take charge of, retain or abandon their churches without previous consultation with their bishop. Any cleric presuming to act contrary to this prohibition was to be punished.[32]

The Decree of Gratian stated that no priest, deacon or anyone else in ecclesiastical orders was allowed to depart from his church in violation of ecclesiastical legislation. They likewise were not to be received into any church. Moreover they were to be forced to report to the church formerly entrusted to them. If they did not return, they were to be excommunicated.[33] Consequently, it seems to have been the mind of Panormitanus that if a cleric could not leave his church and go to another without his bishop's approval, (and if he did, he could be recalled), so also if he happened to join the religious life in like manner he could be recalled.

Other Decretalists arrived practically at the same conclusion, but through a different line of reasoning. Hostiensis († 1271) did not allow a religious to transfer if the Church would suffer serious harm or infamy. If the religious did transfer anyway, he could be recalled. So too could a cleric.[34] In other words, the ancient law was interpreted in the light of Innocent III's canon *Licet*.

By what authority or legal force this revocation of the cleric was effected is not entirely clear. Apparently the abbot would be asked to send the priest as a monk back to the church which had suffered the loss or injury.[35] But whether any legal force could be used against the monastery was not even mentioned.

[32] C. 4, X, *de renuntiatione*, lib. I, tit. 9; JL, n. 14116.

[33] C. 23, C. VII, q. 1.

[34] Lib. III, tit. 31, c. 18, nn. 5, 10 and 16; Joannes Andreae, lib. III, tit. 31, c. 18, n. 22.

[35] C. 5, X, *de statu monachorum*, III, 35.

C. The Admission of Prelates Lower than Bishops

In the decretal *Licet*, Pope Innocent III directed that no bishop may ever desert his office under any pretext whatsoever (not even to embrace the monastic state) without permission obtained from the Roman Pontiff. In his case, teaching was to be preferred to silence, solicitude to contemplation, labor to quietude. What about an abbot if there was a desire to join a stricter Order or to embrace the monastic state? Were they also required to seek and obtain the permission of the Roman Pontiff? On this point the decretalists were not agreed. Joannes Andreae said that to him it appeared that such prelates could fulfill their intentions if they had asked, yet not obtained, the Pope's consent. He maintained that the direction was given to bishops and that the presumption therefore was in the favor of the inferior prelates.[36] On the other hand, he established an argument to the contrary in referring to an instance in which the abbot of Hereford had transferred to a stricter monastery not only without the permission of the Roman Pontiff, or his legate, but even without requesting the same. When rebuked for this mode of action by the Papal legates, the abbot defended himself on the ground that this was the custom in Germany. Pope Innocent III, upon hearing this, replied that such a custom was inimical to the canons (*inimica canonibus*). Therefore the Pope demanded that the custom be no longer observed.[37] Against this, Aegidius still maintained that such a prelate could do it because the law of God is superior to that of the Pope.[38]

Hostiensis at first held the obligation to be doubtful, but later he thought that the permission had to be obtained.

[36] He based his argument on c. 5, X, *de praesumptionibus*, II, 23.

[37] C. 7, X, *de consuetudine*, I, 4; Potthast, n. 3397.

[38] This Decretalist is quoted by Joannes Andreae, lib. III, tit. 31, c. 18, n. 15; the reference probably was to Aegidius de Fuscarariis (†1289).

He reasoned from the fact that, as a subdeacon ordained by the Pope could not receive further Orders from another bishop, so neither should an abbot, or any other prelate inferior to the bishop, transfer to a stricter community, or join the religious life, unless he had asked and received the Pope's permission.[39]

Panormitanus approached the question in a different way. He distinguished between an abbot subject immediately to the Pope, and an abbot subject to another below the Pope. In the former case, it was necessary to ask and receive the permission. In the latter case, to ask was sufficient.[40]

ARTICLE 3. THE TEACHING OF ST. THOMAS AQUINAS

St. Thomas († 1274) repeated a canon of the Decree of Gratian: "If a man while governing the people in his church under the bishop and leading a secular life, is inspired by the Holy Ghost to desire to work out his salvation in a monastery or under some canonical rule, even though his bishop withstand him, we authorize him to go freely."[41] He agreed that the obligation of a perpetual vow came before every other obligation, that religious and bishops were bound by such vows and that the Pope alone could grant them a dispensation. Yet the parish priests and archdeacons were not bound by a perpetual and solemn vow to retain the care of souls. They were free to renounce in the hands of the bishop the charge entrusted to them, because they had not bound themselves to retain their archdeanery or parish forever. He concluded: "Therefore it is evident that archdeacons and parish priests may law-

[39] Quoted by Joannes Andreae, *loc. cit.*

[40] Lib. III, tit. 31, c. 18, n. 13.

[41] C. 2, C. XIX, q. 2. The translation is taken from the *Summa Theologica,* English translation by the Fathers of the English Dominican Province (3 vols., Benziger Brothers, Inc., 1948), IIa-IIae, q. 189, a. 7.

fully enter religion."[42] This opinion was confirmed by Saint Antoninus (1389-1459), who added that the bishop's refusal and opposition could not prevent such action.[43]

[42] *Summa Theologica, loc. cit.*

[43] *Sancti Antonini Summa Theologica in Quattuor Partes distributa* (Verona, 1740), part. 3, tit. 16, cap. 2, §2.

CHAPTER III

FREEDOM OF CLERICS TO ENTER RELIGION AFTER THE COUNCIL OF TRENT

The legislation as found in the Decree of Gratian and in the Decretals of Pope Gregory IX in this regard remained substantially unchanged to the middle of the eighteenth century. The Council of Trent made no reference to the liberty of clerics to enter the religious life. The council did, however, subject to anathema every person of whatever state or dignity, clerics or lay, secular or religious, who would impede without a just cause a virgin or any other woman from either receiving the veil or pronouncing the vows of religion. Not only was this to be observed in respect to such monasteries as were subject to the bishop, but with reference to all monasteries.[1] As it was the final reason of the Tridentine law, according to some authors, to protect the freedom of those who aspired to the religious life and profession, they would have extended this penalty also against those same persons who would prevent any male candidate in a similar case.[2] But since the law was an odious one, a strict interpretation was to be given it and an extension to other cases was not allowed.[3] One reason for the lack of additional legislation on this point may have consisted in the small number of clerics who actually did desire to transfer from the secular to the religious state, while the tendency to leave the cloister in favor of the secular life was greater, which certainly was true two centuries later.[4]

[1] Sess. XXV, *de regularibus*, 18—*Canones et Decreta Concilii Tridentini* (ex editione Romana 1834 repetiti, Neapoli, 1859).

[2] Piatus Montensis, *Praelectiones Iuris Regularis* (3. ed., 2 vols., Parisiis, *imprimatur* 1906), I, 45.

[3] Reg. 15 et 49, R. J. in VI°—*Liber Sextus Decretalium D. Bonifacii Papae VIII suae integritati una cum Clementinis et Extravagantibus earumque Glossis restitutis* (Romae, 1582); Piatus, *Praelectiones Iuris Regularis, loc. cit.*

[4] Benedictus XIV, ep. *Ex quo*, 14 ian. 1747, §22—*Fontes*, n. 374.

ARTICLE 1. BENEDICT XIV'S ATTITUDE IN AN ARCHDEACON'S CASE

On January 14, 1747, Pope Benedict XIV (1740-1758) issued a lengthy and clarifying letter, *Ex quo,* to Cardinal Quirini, which summarized previous legislation and explained in what manner other possible difficulties should preferably be solved. The particular occasion was the entrance of the Archdeacon Leander Chizzola of the Cathedral church of Brescia into the Jesuit monastery, entirely unexpected and without any previous consultation with his local ordinary, Cardinal Quirini. Thereafter the Cardinal wrote to Rome on two different occasions, and once visited the Holy Father personally, and bewailed the Archdeacon's departure which inevitably would cause serious harm to the works of piety and charity among the poor in the diocese in which he had been so actively engaged. The Archdeacon, he said, was already seventy years old and therefore could hope to do little of any use in the Society, and too he was responsible for the upbringing and education of his nephews who were minors. Furthermore, the Cardinal urged the Pope to use his authority in forbidding secular priests and clerics to enter the monastic walls, at least before consulting their bishops. This proposed consultation, the Cardinal stated, would be somewhat similar to the necessary consent as contained in the dismissorial letters of the regular superior that the ordaining bishop must have before the ordination of a religious.[5]

To this formal complaint of the Cardinal, Pope Benedict XIV answered that he knew of no better solution in this special case at hand than the one given by Pope Gregory the Great in a similar case between Bishop Desiderius in Gaul and a deacon Pancratius,[6] who had great abilities and was held in high esteem. But he too had betaken himself to a monastery from which his bishop wanted to recall him. Upon Pancratius' recourse to Rome, Pope Gregory told the

[5] Ep. *Ex quo,* §1.

[6] *Supra,* p. 4.

bishop that this cleric should rather be encouraged to remain in the monastery, lest he be exposed to the dangers of the world once more.[7] Now, although Cardinal Quirini had advanced reasons for keeping the Archdeacon in the service of the diocese, he was to consider himself under the obligation of permitting his cleric to remain in the Jesuit monastery.[8]

Another point which the Roman Pontiff emphasized was that the Archdeacon's neglect to seek the Cardinal's consent was not to be attributed to any lack of due respect towards his ecclesiastical superior, but rather to a reverential fear, an ardent desire of fulfilling his design and a just alarm lest he be prevented in some manner.[9] Accordingly the Pope did not at all seem averse to the Archdeacon's method of entering the religious life without having previously asked his superior's consent.[10]

Article 2. General Legislation

A. Restatement of the Former Law

In regard to Cardinal Quirini's petition for the enactment of additional legislation for the future, Pope Benedict XIV responded that sufficient provisions had been laid down in previous ecclesiastical canons as found in the IV

[7] Ep. *Ex quo,* §2.

[8] Ep.. *Ex quo,* §4

[9] As if to justify the Archdeacon's procedure due to fear, the Pope related a like incident in which Cardinal Ardidinus entered a religious Order with the permission of the Holy Father but without mentioning his proposal to the College of Cardinals. The Cardinal's manner of proceeding was attributed to the fact that he might be hindered by some one in this holy purpose.—Ep. *Ex quo,* §5, in which Pope Benedict stated that this letter of Cardinal Ardicinus to Pope Innocent VIII can be found in his biography edited by Attichy in the book entitled *Flores Sacri Collegii S. R. E. Cardinalium.*

[10] It is to be noted that Pope Benedict was quite exact in demanding that a cleric inform his bishop of the intention to join the religious state. This latter obligation the same Pope treated in his letter, *Ex quo,* §13, and will be discussed in connection with the cleric's duty of consultation with his bishop.

Council of Toledo (633),[11] in the Decree of Gratian[12] and in the collection of the Decretals of Gregory IX. [13] He interpreted this liberty of the clerics to apply equally to beneficed clerics so that, relinquishing their benefice, they might freely enter a monastery, although the bishop objected to their entrance. He based this conclusion on the words of Urban II:

> Si quis horum [clericorum] in Ecclesia sua sub Episcopo populum retinet, et seculariter vivit, si afflatus Spiritu Sancto, in aliquo monasterio vel regulari canonia salvare se voluerit, quia lege privata ducitur, nulla ratio exigit, ut lege publica obstingatur; dignior est enim lex privata, quam pubilca, etc. Quisquis igitur hoc spiritu ducitur, etiam Episcopo suo contradicente, eat liber nostra auctoritate.[14]

For the sake of further clarification of the principle of Benedict XIV, it is helpful to note what Bouix († 1870) had to say as to its application. He was very specific in stating that not only the beneficed clergy were included, but also those of the clergy who were engaged in the care of souls, and that hence a cleric of either group could enter religion without the bishop's consent, even if he was opposed to the entrance. Bouix stated that all Catholic writers were in agreement on this point.[15] St. Alphonsus Liguori († 1787) particularly included a pastor as having this right, and held with St. Thomas Aquinas that it was foolish to fear that all pastors would join the religious life and that thereby the souls of the faithful would soon be forsaken.[16]

[11] *Supra*, p. 3.

[12] *Supra*, pp. 8 and 9.

[13] *Supra*, pp. 11-15.

[14] Ep. *Ex quo*, §6.

[15] D. Bouix, *Tractatus de Jure Regularium* (2 vols., Parisiis, 1857), I, 542-544 (hereafter cited as *De Jure Regularium*).

[16] *Theologia Moralis* (ed. novissima, 6 vols., Parisiis, no date), lib. V, cap. 1, n. 74; Vermeersch says the same concerning pastors.—*De Religiosis Institutis et Personis*, I, (Brugis: sumptibus Beyaert, 1902), n. 136 (hereafter cited as *De Religiosis Institutis*). Cf. F. X Wernz, *Ius Decretalium*, Vol. III (2. ed., Romae, 1908), Pars II, n. 629.

B. The Teaching of the Doctors of the Church

To strengthen his argument Pope Benedict asserted with St. Thomas Aquinas that a cleric was not bound by any law to devote his entire life to the care of souls, but only for as long as he retained a parish. And he was not obliged to remain perpetually in the service of a parish.[17]

Guarding against any possible interpretation which would restrict this liberty of clerics to enter only institutes of monks, Pope Benedict XIV cited Sylvius († 1649), who affirmed that this opportunity belonged to clerics who wanted to enter not only those institutes that were engaged solely in contemplation but equally to those that were engaged in works of the active life, because the state of religion excelled the state or rather the office of an archdeacon as the state of the highest religion excelled that of the lowest.[18]

This was to be said truthfully and correctly because of the solemn vows (*solemnia vota*) of chastity, poverty and obedience which are pronounced in religious institutes.[19]

The fact that a cleric might licitly enter a monastery even though his bishop refused permission should not be a cause of wonderment, Pope Benedict asserted, for although a cleric at his ordination had promised respect and obedience, so a religious too, through the profession of vows, promised more solemnly a like obedience to his superior. Yet such a professed religious desirous of transferring to a stricter community, after having requested permission for the transfer from his superior in the less strict community, might freely depart to fulfill his purpose

[17] Ep. *Ex quo*, §7; the citation of St. Thomas Aquinas is found in *Summa Theologica*, IIa-IIae, q. 189, a. 7.

[18] "...quoniam plus excedit status Religionis cuiuscumque, statum seu potius officium Archidiaconi vel Plebani, quam status altissimae Religionis, statum cuiuscumque infimae."—*Ex quo*, §§7, 8. This citation of the theologian is found in his work: F. Sylvius, *Commentarium in Summam Sancti Thomae* (3. ed., 6 vols., Antverpiae, 1667), IIa-IIae, q. 189, a. 7 (hereafter cited as Sylvius).

[19] Ep. *Ex quo*, §8.

even though this superior refused to grant him leave. For whenever a prelate misuses his given authority by such a bold and indiscreet opposition, this same superior deserves to lose his privilege or right in this regard.[20]

Article 3. Consultation between the Bishop and the Religious Superior

Pope Benedict XIV acknowledged the complaint of Cardinal Quirini that on account of extraordinary circumstances some difficulties would advise against a granting of the sought permission, that it was necessary to examine and look into such unusual events, and that a papal Constitution demanding a consultation between the bishop and religious superior would contribute immensely toward solving such problems. But such counsel had never been forbidden in the past, and the Pope insinuated that it could be employed most fittingly and usefully. However, to enforce it through enactment of law would be not a little impractical. Nor had this legal caution been found necessary in respect to the two religious superiors when the subject of one wished to transfer to the other's community. Only when a controversy arose whether the transfer to the stricter community was sought from a praiseworthy reason or rather out of levity and inconstancy, was the judgment of a higher superior required by ecclesiastical law. After the religious subject had made known and proved his intentions to the Holy See, the Roman Pontiff granted him leave for the transfer which would include also the permission of the superior of the less strict community.[21]

Article 4. Entrance into Religious on the Part of Prelates Inferior to Bishops

In general, prelates inferior to bishops were said to have the same liberty to enter religion as other clerics even

[20] Ep. *Ex quo*, §14.
[21] Ep. *Ex quo*, §§16 and 17.

if their request to live a higher life in a monastery was denied by their bishop. Suarez († 1617) held that theirs was not a bond which of its nature could not be broken for the sake of greater perfection, nor were they prevented from so doing by any human law.[22]

Fagnanus († 1678) stated that if such a prelate was a subject to a superior below the Pope, he could claim to have the same right as other clerics in this respect. However, an exempt prelate could not abandon his prelacy, nor transfer to a stricter institute unless he had previously obtained from the Pope the permission requested of him, and this on account of the bond of prelacy (*vinculum Praelaturae*).[23] Then he proceeded in the same train of thought holding that an inferior prelate either had a superior below that of the Pope himself, and in this case a mere request for the desired consent, although the permission were not given, would suffice, or the inferior prelate was immediately subject to the Pope, and in this case he could not pass to the religious state if the Pope refused his permission. Should the Pope not respond at all, and the prelate make the transfer, it would indeed be valid but might be the cause of some displeasure since the Pope could recall him.[24]

Tamburini († 1666), Abbot-general of the Vallombrasion Benedictines, referred to inferior prelates as having quasi-episcopal jurisdiction in a diocese *pleno iure* subjected to them and stated that these must be considered as bishops in regard to this right, because in all things concerning jurisdiction they were to be treated as bishops, differing only from the latter in episcopal consecration. Yet they were true spouses of their churches. Wherefore they were

[22] F. Suarez, *Opera Omnia,* tom. XV (ed. nova, Parisiis, 1859), lib. V, cap. 4, n. 14.

[23] P. Fagnanus, *Commentaria in Quinque Libros Decretalium,* Vol. III (Venetiis, 1709), c. 18, X, *de regularibus et transeuntibus ad religionem,* III, 31, n. 41.

[24] *Ibid.,* n. 42, in which he based his argument on that of Joannes Andreae in cap. *Cum non stat.,* nn. 11 and 12, *de regul. iur.* lib. 6 *in Mercurialibus.*

not allowed to join the religious life without the consent of the Apostolic See.[25]

ARTICLE 5. THE RIGHT OF CONGREGATIONS IN ACCEPTING CLERICAL CANDIDATES

By a strict application of the cleric's freedom as asserted in the letter, *Ex quo,* some authors held that it referred only to those clerics who intended to enter a monastery where solemn vows were pronounced. In the course of time, on account of the similarity of reasons and by analogy, the principle was extended also to congregations wherein simple vows were made.[26] To dispel all difficulties in this matter, however, the Holy See was asked whether the Congregation of secular priests, namely, the Oblates of the Blessed Virgin, who pronounced simple vows only, might also receive clerics whose entrance into religion was opposed by their bishop. The Sacred Congregation of Bishops and Regulars on June 28, 1837, replied that the state of religion was of greater security towards salvation even in approved institutes in which simple vows were made,[27] and that therefore the same reason was present for which Pope Benedict XIV allowed the entrance into an Order of regulars. The answer was: "Affirmative, ne impediatur vocatio ad statum perfectiorem."[28]

[25] A. Tamburini de Marradio, *De Iure Abbatum et Aliorum Praelatorum* (3 vols., Lugduni, 1640), III, disp. VI, q. III, nn. 7 and 8; T. Sanchez, *Opus Morale in Praecepta Decalogi* (2 vols., Lugduni, 1661), lib. IV, cap. 25, n. 49 (hereafter cited as *Opus Morale*).

[26] H. I. Icard, *Praelectiones Juris Canonici habitae in seminario Sancti Sulpitii* (6. ed., 3 vols., Parisiis, 1886), vol. II, sec. 5, art. 4, n. 460 (hereafter cited as *Praelectiones Juris Canonici*). The author was the Superior-general of the Sulpicians from 1875-1893.

[27] Pope Leo XIII approved the Constitutions of the Oblates of the Blessed Virgin Mary on Sept. 1, 1826—S. C. Ep. et Reg., *Pinerolien.*, 28 iun. 1837—*Fontes,* n. 1914.

[28] S. C. Ep. et Reg., *loc. cit.;* Bouix, *op. cit.,* I, 548, 549; Wernz, *Ius Decretalium,* Vol. III, Pars II, n. 629.

CHAPTER IV

DOUBTFUL OBLIGATION OF ASKING BISHOP'S CONSENT

Article 1. Affirmative and Negative Arguments

The fact that a cleric was not to be denied entrance into religion on account of the opposition of his bishop raised the question among authors whether the cleric was even obliged to make the request for his bishop's consent. Bouix[1] and Schmalzgrueber († 1735)[2] agreed that the question was a doubtful one. For the affirmative side there was St. Alphonsus Liguori, who, although he did not mention the problem in so many words, implied that a cleric should seek this consent from his bishop when he taught that a cleric could disregard the refusal of his bishop when the latter gave a negative reply to the petition.[3]

A similar implication that the petition should be addressed to the bishop is found in the writings of St. Thomas Aquinas. Having mentioned that the obligation of perpetual vows stood before every other obligation, he stated that bishops and religious are bound by such perpetual vows to devote themselves to the divine service, while parish priests and archdeacons were not bound, as bishops are, by a perpetual vow to retain the care of souls. Wherefore bishops cannot abandon their bishopric on any pretext whatsoever without the authority of the Roman Pontiff. But archdeacons and parish priests are free to renounce into the hands of the bishops the charge entrusted to them, without the Pope's special permission, who alone

[1] *De Jure Regularium,* I, 548.

[2] F. Schmalzgrueber, *Jus Ecclesiasticum Universum* (5 vols. bound in 12, Romae, 1843-1845), Lib. III, tit. 31, n. 34 (hereafter cited as *Jus Ecclesiasticum*).

[3] *Theologia Moralis,* lib. 5, cap. 1, n. 74; Piatus (1815-1904) cited St. Alphonsus de Liguori as of the affirmative opinion—*Praelectiones Iuris Regularis,* I, 79.

can dispense from perpetual vows. These clerics can do this, he argued, even if their bishop withstood them.[4]

Another author, according to Schmalzgrueber,[5] who seemed to hold the affirmative opinion was Azorius († 1603), who referred to the question under discussion only indirectly.

> An clerici in dignitate Ecclesiastica constituti vel animarum curae praefecti, vel beneficium habentes, quod residentiam clerici iure communi requirit, quales sunt parochi, archipresbyteri, archdiaconi, decani, praepositi, priores, canonici, ac similes aliquid vovere possint?

And he answered:

> ... fas esse cuilibet ecclesiae praefecto, vel clerico praeter episcopum, deposita cura, vel dignitate, aut eccelsiastico beneficio legitime, et rite abdicato, vel etiam cura, et dignitate, beneficio nondum depositis, religiosam vitam suscipere: ... id eis concedi etiam Episcopo contradicente; petita tamen facultate, quamvis non obtenta.[6]

As stated previously, Azorius does not mention any obligation on the part of the cleric to request his bishop's consent. He does take for granted that the petition was made.

Among the authors leaning to the negative side, namely, that clerics were not obliged to seek this permission of entering religion, was Suarez. He did not express this same idea precisely, though his opinion can be gathered from the context. He argued that the episcopacy in itself did not prevent entrance into the novitiate, but only when a bishop attempted to do this without the permission of the Pope. Even then it was not to be considered as entirely null, but rather for that length of time only till the necessary

[4] *Summa Theologica,* IIa-IIae, q. 189, a. 7. "Sanctus Thomas... [et Azor] videntur accedere ad affirmativam."—Bouix, *De Jure Regularium,* I, 548.

[5] *Loc. cit.*

[6] Ioannes Azorius, *Institutiones Morales* (3 vols., Brixiae, 1617), pars I, lib. 11, cap. 16, q. 3. "[Sanctus Thomas et] Azor... videntur accedere ad affirmativam."—Bouix, *De Jure Regularium,* I, 548.

condition was fulfilled. From this argument he proceeded to the obligation of inferior prelates and clerics to obtain the permission from their bishop, and stated first that it could be doubted whether they needed this permission at any time. In fact, in his following sentence he held definitely the negative opinion for the reason that there is no bond which of its nature cannot be renounced by inferior prelates and clerics for the sake of a greater perfection, nor were they prohibited by any human law from doing so.[7]

Schmalzgrueber, arriving at a similar conclusion, simply and clearly stated that no law imposed the obligation of seeking this episcopal consent, but added that clerics in charge of the care of souls were obliged to inform their bishop of their act.[8]

Bouix made an evident but worthwhile distinction in averring that to ask permission was one thing, and to inform the bishop of one's proximate departure was quite another.[9]

Sanchez († 1610) mentioned that some authors required that the permission be asked because they were influenced by the canon *Licet,*[10] which referred only to religious who desired a transfer, and he admitted that these must seek the permission. He said it might possibly be argued from the canon *Admonet,*[11] which forbade beneficed clerics to leave their churches without a previous consultation with their bishop. However, no proof in any law could be found that this pertained also to clerics who contemplated joining the religious life, and he expressed his belief that no obligation existed that demanded this petition from such clerics. Otherwise it would be in the bishop's power to decide whether these clerics were motivated by praiseworthy zeal. If he found that zeal lacking, he could refuse the per-

[7] *Opera Omnia,* tom. XV, lib. 5, cap. 4, n. 14; cf. Schmalzgrueber, *Jus Ecclesiasticum, loc. cit.*

[8] *Jus Ecclesiasticum, loc. cit.*

[9] *De Jure Regularium,* I, 548.

[10] *Supra,* p. 13.

[11] *Supra,* p. 17.

mission. In addition he stated that Pope Urban II[12] had conceded absolutely complete freedom to clerical aspirants to transfer to a religious community.[13]

Because of the arguments on both sides as to the obligation, the opinion of Vermeersch (1858-1936), which he held before the promulgation of the Code, is a proper solution: "Probabilius ne petenda quidem est venia Episcopi . . ."[14]

Piatus held that clerics, at least those having the care of souls, were obliged by the precept of the natural law to seek this permission, but he seemingly held this request to be one manner of informing the bishop of an intended transfer to the religious life.[15] But the latter is not the immediate problem under discussion. The obligation upon a clerical aspirant to the religious life of informing his bishop of his intention will be considered in the following article.

Article 2. Obligation of Informing the Bishop

According to the response of Pope Benedict XIV, no reasonable doubt could be maintained concerning the obligation of a pastor about to abandon the ministry and government of a church to make known to his bishop his plans and the reasons for them to the extent their nature allowed. The fulfillment of this duty is demanded, the response insisted, in view of the very uprightness and fidelity which constitute the observance of the natural law. Since priests were engaged in the care of souls and other important offices pertaining to a pastor's guidance and direction, they were ministers of the bishop and consequently were obliged

[12] *Supra*, pp. 10 and 11.

[13] *Opus Morale, ibid.*, n. 48; Lucius Ferraris (†1763) contended that clerics could enter religion without asking any permission of their bishop.—*Prompta Bibliotheca Canonica, Juridica, Moralis, Theologica, necnon Ascetica, Polemica, Rubristica, Historica* (ed. novissima, 9 vols., Romae, 1885-1899), VIII, n. 21. Fagnanus also held the negative opinion without any kind of doubt.—*Commentarium in Tertium Librum Decretalium*, c. 18, X, *de regularibus et transeuntibus ad religionem*, III, 31, n. 28.

[14] *De Religiosis Institutis*, I, n. 135.

[15] Cf. *Praelectiones Iuris Regularis*, I, 79.

to cooperate with him in such a manner that he might opportunely and fittingly provide for the souls for whom they had labored and regarding the affairs which they had administered.[16]

For a further teratment of this obligation Pope Benedict XIV referred to the teaching of Passerini († 1677), who affirmed that a minister who has the custody of the goods of the Lord, if they would perish without his watchfulness and protection, is obliged out of decency and fidelity to duty to return them over to the Lord. Hence he must inform his bishop of his plan in order that the latter may provide through another minister for the care of the pastoral office. Should the pastor have failed to communicate with his bishop on this point, he could be punished. He would sin no less in his negligence than would the bishop himself were he to abandon his flock without providing that another shepherd would take his place. Considering the natural law in itself in respect to this responsibility, Passerini thought it could be possible that such neglect on the part of the pastor would not be a serious sin if he was assured that no imminent danger would result before the bishop was informed through another source of the pastor's departure. Yet from this principle it would not follow that such a departure by its very nature would not be a very grave wrong in itself, because such negligence implies the abandonment of a sheepfold by leaving it without a shepherd amidst the dangers and hazards of the world.[17]

The teaching of Passerini thus far was included in the letter of Benedict XIV by a direct quotation of a part of it and by an approval of the remainder. The same author, however, had more to say in his commentary (which was not mentioned by the Pope), when he extended this obligation of consultation with the bishop also to inferior prelates who wanted to embrace the religious life. He also men-

[16] Ep. *Ex quo*, §13.

[17] Petrus Passerini, *Inspectiones Morales de Statibus Hominum* (3 vols., Lucae, 1732), tom. III, q. 189, a. 7, n. 8 (hereafter cited as *Inspectiones Morales*).

tioned that the office of an archdeacon and pastor and the ministry of souls was a ministerial office to be performed under the direction of the bishop, and an instrumental office but not of itself (*de se*) held in perpetuity. Of its nature it was separable from the incumbent, and only through the provision of positive law did it have any kind of stable characteristic, which however was not so unchangeable as to impede entrance into religion.[18]

Having argued and agreed that a cleric had no obligation in law to seek the consent of his bishop for entering religion, Schmalzgrueber added that a beneficed cleric or one having the care of souls was bound to inform his bishop of his intention beforehand. At least after he had departed from his charge would he be obliged to do this, so that his deserted flock might be properly provided for.[19]

According to the mind of St. Alphonsus Liguori, the information had to be conveyed to the bishop before the cleric had attempted to seek admittance to the institute, though in an exceptional case a cleric might not sin if he entered without any notice sent to his bishop in view of a reverential fear that he might be prevented from the pursuit of his desire.[20]

An additional observation favoring the cleric's obligation to inform his bishop was advanced by Bouix, namely, the resulting opportunities that the bishop had, in case he considered the cleric unfit for the religious life, of informing the religious superior of this shortcoming. It would be wrong to suppose that a bishop could not advise his clerics or the religious superiors in such matters.[21]

Not only must a pastor inform his bishop of his future plan in this regard, but Piatus insisted that he must also

[18] *Ibid.*, nn. 9 and 10.

[19] *Jus Ecclesiasticum, op. cit.*, Lib. III, tit. 31, n. 34. Franciscus Schmier (†1728) held the same opinion.—*Jurisprudentia Canonico-Civilis* (2 vols., Venetiis, 1754), tom. II, tr. 1, pars 1, cap. 3, n. 95.

[20] Theologia Moralis, lib. 5, cap. 1, n. 75. For the exceptional instance he based his argument on the letter of Benedict XIV, *ex quo*, §5.

[21] *De Jure Regularium*, I, 546.

delay his departure for some time, not necessarily for an extensive period, so that his bishop might be afforded an opportunity of sending another in his place for the parishioners.[22]

Because of the response of Pope Benedict XIV and the almost unanimous agreement of the authors, there can hardly be a doubt that ordinarily not only beneficed clerics, including archdeacons and even those lower in dignity, for no distinction was made in regard to the cleric's rank, but also priests to whom had been entrusted the care of souls were required to inform their bishop of their departure in due time so that he would be able to make arrangements for the care of the flock before it suffered serious harm. The only difficulty remaining on this point it whether this same obligation could have been said to bind clerics ordained under a title different from that of a benefice, or clerics not charged with the actual ministry of souls. A solution to this question was advanced by Bouix, who mentioned that clerics in general had this obligation, so that they might enable their bishop to appoint another one of the clergy to perform the work and function left undone by the former's departure.[23] Larraona in more precise terms held the same opinion when he stated that the moral obligation of advising the ordinary in a matter of such importance was incumbent upon every cleric, and especially on a cleric who had a benefice or who was entrusted with the care of souls.[24]

The fulfillment of the obligation of approaching their bishop on the part of the clerical candidates for the religious life had been rendered relatively simple and easy by the legislation in the common law which directed the

[22] Piatus, *Praelectiones Iuris Regularis,* I, 79. Cf. Vermeersch, *De Religiosis Institutis,* I, nn. 135, 136.

[23] *De Jure Regularium,* I, 546.

[24] "Commentarium Codicis," *Commentarium pro Religiosis* (later [1935], *Commentarium pro Religiosis et Missionariis*), (Romae, 1920—), XVII (1936), 242 (hereafter cited as *CpRM* from 1935 onward).

obtaining of testimonial letters before admittance to the religious habit.[25]

ARTICLE 3. TESTIMONIAL LETTERS AS A MEANS OF INFORMING THE BISHOP

On January 25, 1848, Pope Pius IX enacted the first definite legislation in regard to the necessity of obtaining testimonial letters. He thought it best that the local ordinary should be asked about the candidates' qualities because the same ordinary, in virtue of his pastoral office, would know his sheep better than anyone else and oftentimes would be aware of impediments hidden to others. After consulting the Cardinals of the proper Sacred Congregation, the Pope commanded that the following be observed everywhere and for all times: that no candidate be admitted into the religious life without testimonial letters from the local ordinary of the diocese of his origin and from every local ordinary in whose diocese the candidate lived for more than a year after the completion of his fifteenth year. This applied whether the candidate sought admission into an Order, a Congregation, a Society, an Institute, a Monastery, or a House, whether solemn or simple vows were pronounced therein, regardless of any particular privilege or any other title by which exemption from general decrees might be enjoyed (unless a special, individual and express mention was made of such exemption).[26]

The ordinaries after diligent and perhaps even secret inquiry were obliged to inform the religious superiors concerning the candidate's origin, birthplace, age, life, morals, reputation, condition, education and learning. They were to note whether the candidate was impeded by some censure, irregularity, or other canonical impediment, and whether

[25] Wernz, *Ius Decretalium,* Vol. III, pars II, n. 629; Piatus, *Praelectiones Iuris Regularis,* I, p. 78. It is true that the bishop is thereby informed of the cleric's future entrance into religion, but that does not meet the requirement of consultation. *Infra,* pp. 91-116.

[26] S. C. super Statu Regularium, decr. *Romani Pontifices,* 25 ian. 1848, §I—*Fontes,* n. 4375.

he was burdened with debts or bound to render an account in regard to any business administration. This obligation was said to bind the ordinaries in conscience, so that never were they free to refuse these same testimonial letters.[27]

On the other hand, the Pope commanded that all religious superiors of whatever rank, even of exempt or privileged institutes, should observe this decree by obtaining the aforementioned letters. He imposed this mandate as binding under the vow of obedience. Whosoever among them would receive a candidate to the religious habit contrary to the tenor of this decree would by that very fact be deprived of all offices, of the right to vote, and of the ability to obtain any office in the future. From this penalty the Apostolic See alone could dispense.[28]

No mitigation of this decree was ever to be presumed in virtue of any kind of privilege, faculty, indult, dispensation, approval of rules and constitutions, which an Order, Institute, superior or another religious might obtain from the Holy See, unless the decree was derogated expressly by name. Should an institute ever receive such an unusual dispensation, it could not be extended to other institutes by any sort of privilege or communication. Pope Pius IX ordered that this decree be read in public on the first of January of each year under penalty of the superior's *ipso facto* effected privation of office, of the right of voting and eligibility for office.[29]

In consideration of the wide scope and severity of this decree, it is difficult to conceive how thereafter any clerical candidate could possibly enter a religious institute without the bishop's knowledge.

About ten years later this law was altered slightly in regard to clerics in major orders, so that for them it sufficed to have testimonial letters from their ordaining bishop and from that local ordinary in whose diocese the cleric

[27] *Ibid.*, §II.
[28] *Ibid.*, §III.
[29] *Ibid.*, §§IV, V.

resided for more than one year. The proposed question was as follows:

> Si sia sufficiente di esigere dai Postulanti ecclesiastici le lettere testimoniali del Vescovo che gli ha conferito l'ordine, ovvero, sia necessaria anche la testimoniale del Vescovo nelle cui Diocesi sono stati ultimamente impiegati?

To which this response was given:

> Si agatur de postulantibus in Sacris Ordinibus constitutis, sufficere testimoniales Episcopi, qui Ordines Sacros legitime eis contulit, una cum testimonialibus Ordinariorum Dioecesum, in quibus deinde ultra annum in unaquaque Dioecesi commorati fuerint.[30]

This response is indicated as a source for canon 544, §4, in the Code of Canon Law (promulgated on Pentecost, 1917) and the canon reads:

> Pro clericis admittendis, praeter testimonium ordinationis, sufficiunt litterae testimoniales Ordinariorum in quorum dioecesibus post ordinationem ultra annum moraliter continuum sint commorati, salvo praescripto §3.

This obligation was extended, therefore, to all clerics. Canon 108, §1, included as *clerici* those assigned to the sacred ministry by the first tonsure.

However stringent the demand and legislation for testimonial letters, Bouix remarked that this restriction did not interfere with the freedom of clerics to enter religion even if the bishop should be opposed to their departure. The decree of Pope Pius IX did not mention, much less demand, the bishop's permission or approval as a necessary requisite. Neither were regular superiors forbidden by this decree to receive such clerical candidates should their bishop be opposed.[31]

History reports an interesting event concerning this manner of procedure which turned out disagreeably for both

[30] S. C. super Statu Regularium, declar. 29 maii 1857—*Fontes*, n. 4382.

[31] *De Jure Regularium*, I, 552.

parties. On September 23, 1885, the Sacred Congregation of Bishops and Regulars responded to a certain ordinary in Spain who had opposed a priest's entrance into a religious Congregation:

> Pro relaxatione litterarum testimonialium favore . . . oratoris ad tramites Decreti Romani Pontifices 25 Jan. 1848, facta prius ab eo, erga proprium Episcopum, decenti excusatione. Declaravit insuper nullam censuram Episcopi et Curiam obligavit ad damnum Oratori compensandum ex censura et beneficii privatione ortum.[32]

By way of conclusion in this chaper, it must be admitted that the duty of seeking the local ordinary's consent remained a doubtful obligation. The common practice was that the cleric would at least inform his ordinary of his desired transfer to the religious state. This information was extended to him either prior to the cleric's departure from the diocese to enter religion, or at least at the time when the request for the testimonial letters was made.

[32] Cf. Boletin Religioso de la Congregacion de Misioneros Hijos del C. de Maria (Madrid), I (1886), 9, as given by Larraona, "Commentarium Codicis," *CpRM*, XVII (1936), 242, notes 287 and 288.

CHAPTER V

CONFLICTING OBLIGATIONS ARISING FROM VARIOUS CAUSES

In chapter III it was pointed out that ordinarily clerics and prelates inferior to bishops had the liberty to embrace the religious life, a freedom which was not taken away even though their bishop should be opposed to their intention. In relation to this general principle several exceptions arising from other simultaneous obligations exerted some influence. These questions will be treated in the present chapter in connection with the following conflicting obligations:

a) that of clerics who were bound by the oath *ex instituto Sanctae Sedis;*

b) that of clerics who were bound by some contractual obligation;

c) that of clerics who had promised obedience to their bishop;

d) that of clerics burdened with possible restrictions imposed by the bishop;

e) that of clerics whose entrance into religion would result in grave harm to the Church.

ARTICLE 1. THE OATH "EX INSTITUTO SANCTAE SEDIS"

Any cleric who has taken the oath *ex instituto Sanctae Sedis* cannot licitly or validly enter the religious life because, according to canon 542, 1° *ult.*, such an oath constitutes a diriment impediment. This legislation originated November 24, 1625, when Pope Urban VIII (1623-1644) drew up a formula for an oath to be taken by all seminarians over fourteen years of age in the *Collegium Urbanum,* an international Roman seminary which the same Pope established under the supervision of the Sacred Congregation for the Propagation of the Faith for the training of priests for missionary territories.[1] According to the formula of this oath, all the students required to take it promised that after their ordination to the priesthood they would return to their own respective dioceses where they would perpetually labor for the welfare of souls. They also promised not to enter a religious institute, society, or regular congregation without a special permission of the Holy See and the Sacred Congregation for the Propagation of the Faith in particular.[2]

These same students were ordained on a title called the *titulus missionis,* for which a similar oath was necessary. This title, first permitted in the Irish College at Rome in 1631,[4] was permitted later to all colleges which were under the Sacred Congregation for the Propagation of the Faith.[5] Clerics ordained on this title were also obliged to labor among the faithful of their missionary territory. Their sustenance was derived from offerings of the latter. The Sacred Congregation stated on August 7, 1645, that the oath which necessarily accompanied the ordination on the "title of the missions" bound these clerics perpetually to the missions for which they were destined.[6]

On July 20, 1660, Alexander VII (1655-1667) amplified and explained the juridical implications of this oath and ordered that it be taken according to the new formula which he proposed.[7] The prohibition against entering re-

[1] *Collectanea S. Congregationis de Propaganda Fide* (2 vols., Romae: Typographia Polyglotta S. C. de Propaganda Fide, 1907), I, n. 19 (hereafter cited as *Collectanea S. C. P. F.*).

[2] This formula, with later amendments, appears in the *Fontes,* n. 237.

[3] *Collectanea S.C.P.F., loc. cit.*

[4] Pope Urban VIII, const. *Sacrosanctae,* 12 apr. 1631—*Juris Pontificii de Propaganda Fide Complectens Decreta Instructiones Encyclicas Litteras Etc.* (ed. Raphaelis de Martinis, 7 vols., Romae, 1888-1898), P. I, t. 1, p. 128, (hereafter cited as *Jus Pontificium* de P.F.).

[5] Const. *Ad uberes,* 18 maii 1638—De Martinis, *Jus Pontificium de P. F.,* P. I, t. 1, p. 173.

[6] *Collectanea S. C. P. F.,* I, n. 113.

[7] Const. *Cum circa,* 20 iul. 1660, §5—*Fontes,* n. 237.

ligion was contained also in this oath and was considered as binding these students not only while they were in the College of the Propaganda but during their entire life, even though they might have left the College at any time or had been dismissed from it. Regardless of what reason they had for wanting to enter the religious life, the written permission of the Holy See was a necessary requisite.[8] The Sacred Congregation, on April 8, 1661, also declared that the provisions of the bulls originally establishing the various colleges in virtue of which students were allowed to enter the religious life were to be recalled. Yet the Holy See did not intend absolutely to forbid these clerics to enter religion, but rather to reserve the sufficiency of their alleged reasons to the judgment of the Holy See after having heard the ordinary of the territory for which the cleric was destined. In this case the public good was to be preferred to the private good of the individual.[9] Moreover, when the Holy See did grant permission to such a cleric to enter religion, the aspirant was required to enter an institute which was actually engaged in missionary endeavors in the territory which he was previously destined to serve, and there to devote himself perpetually to the work of the salvation of souls.[10]

By special indults from the Holy See, some countries in which the episcopal hierarchy had been established were permitted to use the "title of the mission" in the ordination of clerics for their region. Such indults were received by the Bishops of Canada, England, Scotland, Ireland and the United States, usually for intervals of five years.[11]

The II Plenary Council of Baltimore in 1866 petitioned

[8] *Ibid.*, §2.

[9] De Martinis, *Jus Pontificium de P. F.*, P. II, t. 1, p. 121 ad II et III.

[10] *Ibid.*, ad IV.

[11] Cf. Conc. Provinc. Balt. III (1837), *Decreta*, n. 1, apud Mansi, XXXIX, 349. Indultum Sacrae Congregationis de Propaganda Fide, 3 oct. 1852—Mansi, XLIV, 689. *Concilii Plenarii Baltimorensis II, Acta et Decreta* (Baltimorae: Murphy, 1868), tit. III, cap. ii, n. 89.

the Holy See to permit the ordination of clerics on the title of "service of the missions" without the usually required oath, because many were reluctant to take it and the oath did not seem any longer necessary to obtain the ends for which it was originally demanded.[12] The Sacred Congregation for the Propagation of the Faith responded on January 24, 1868, demanding that all clerics ordained on this title must, before their ordination to the subdiaconate, take the oath, according to the manner of Pontifical students, whereby they promise to serve their diocese or mission perpetually.[13]

On April 27, 1871, an Instruction of this Congregation, in respect to the discipline governing various titles of ordination, went on to explain that any cleric ordained in virtue of an Apostle Indult on the "title of the mission"[14] was required before his ordination to take the oath according to the prescribed formula contained in the Instruction itself. Patterned after that of Popes Urban VIII (1623-1644) and Alexander VII (1655-1667), it obliged the cleric to perpetual service for souls in that diocese or mission territory which the candidate swore to serve. It also prevented his entering religion without the permission of the Holy See, and in particular of the Sacred Congregation for the Propagation of the Faith, to whom it pertained (after hearing the ordinary) to decide whether he could be spared.[15]

Hence not only those students who had been educated at the College of the Propaganda in Rome, but all clerics ordained anywhere in the world on the "title of the mission" fell under the direct authority of the Holy See. This oath thus pronounced by these clerics certainly derived

[12] *Concilii Plenarii Baltimorensis II, Acta et Decreta,* tit. V, cap. VIII, n. 323.

[13] *Concilii Plenarii Baltimorensis II, Acta et Decreta, op. cit.,* p. cxlvii.

[14] Instructio Sacrae Congregationis de Propaganda Fide de Titulo Ordinationis—*Collectanea S.C.P.F.,* I, n. 1369, §§6, 7.

[15] *Ibid.,* §§8 and 10.

ex instituto Sanctate Sedis, since the Sacred Congregation for the Propagation of the Faith alone could release them from their obligations either when they transferred from one diocese to another or when they entered the religious life.[16]

In 1908 Pope Pius X (1903-1914) removed England, Scotland, Ireland, Canada and the United States from the jurisdiction of the Sacred Congregation for the Propagation of the Faith and placed them under the Sacred Consistorial Congregation.[17] On August 6 of the following year the Sacred Consistorial Congregation stated that students of these countries who were attending the Pontifical College of the Propaganda in Rome were to be ordained under the title of the "service of the church" if no other title were possible, and they were to continue to take the oath prescribed by Popes Urban VIII and Alexander VII according to a newly prescribed formula.[18] Asked whether clerics of the United States, in view of the Indult granted to this country to ordained clerics on the "title of service of the church or diocese, the Sacred Congregation responded:

> Negative, nisi ad id adigantur in casibus a iure communi praescriptis; facta tamen obligatione alumnis, qui gratuito in bonum dioecesis aluntur, promissionem scriptam emittendi, sese fideliter inservituros esse propriae dioecesi.[19]

Hence it appears that, among the students of the countries that were removed from the Sacred Congregation of the Propagation of the Faith and placed under the Sacred Consistorial Congregation, only those students who were educated in the Urban College in Rome were bound to take this oath under the formula of 1909. Hence only they could

[16] James V. Brown, *Non-Age, Fear, Fraud, Crime and Oath "ex Instituto Sanctae Sedis," as Diriment Impediments to Entrance into the Novitiate,* The Catholic University of America Canon Law Studies (Washington, D.C.; The Catholic University of America Press, 1949, unpublished), p. 163; cf. *ibid.,* pp. 157-165.

[17] Const. *Sapienti consilio,* 29 iun. 1908—*Fontes,* n. 682.

[18] S.C. Consist., *Romana,* 6 aug. 1909, ad XIII—*Fontes,* n. 2061.

[19] *Ibid.,* ad XIV.

be said properly to have an oath *ex instituto Sanctae Sedis,* which on that score constituted a diriment impediment to their entering religion. The English College at Lisbon was to continue to use the original oath prescribed by Popes Urban VIII and Alexander VII, as were the students in Rome from countries remaining under the Sacred Congregation for the Propagation of the Faith.[20] Those clerics, therefore, who had taken the oath *ex instituto Sanctae Sedis* in accordance with any of the prescribed formulae approved at the time were not free to enter religion when they desired, but had to receive special permission from the Holy See.

ARTICLE 2. SINGULAR CONTRACT BINDING CLERIC TO SERVICE OF DIOCESE

Although a cleric fundamentally had the liberty to embrace the religious life, he may have been forbidden the exercise thereof on account of some previous agreement or contract with his bishop or diocese and for the length of time required for the satisfaction of this contractual obligation. Such an agreement or contract can possibly have arisen from the use of funds and donations destined for the support and education of a cleric who would work in a specified territory where priests were badly needed. Young men who wish to accept this financial assistace may bind themselves to the bishops of the defined diocese for a certain number of years. In this manner were educated many of the candidates for the priesthood in the schools, of England, Germany and other countries. To these clerics entrance into religion before the completion of the promised number of years was not allowed. The reason given for this was that the embracing of the religious life was binding only as a counsel whereas the fulfillment of a contract was binding under precept.[21]

Whether or not students in either a minor or a major seminary (in France) should be considered as held by the

[20] *Ibid.*, ad XIII.

[21] Bouix, *De Jure Regularium,* I, 550.

term of such a contract, at least when it was a tacit contract, presented a difficulty of which a solution was not quite clear to a nineteenth century canonist, Bouix. At first, he maintained an affirmative opinion, but upon a deeper study of the question he became doubtful whether an obligation was imposed upon the student and sought the advice of a prudent and learned contemporary. The latter presented reasons favoring the negative opinion. These reasons were:[22]

a) The aforementioned donations and funds were not given with the condition that if a seminarian would not advance to major orders he would be obliged to repayment, but the student was at liberty to remain even in the lay state, for there were a number of precedents in which such students had quit their pursuit of clerical studies without any recompense having been demanded by the donors;

b) Since these donors apparently consented to a seminarian's choice of remaining in the lay state if he desired, *a fortiori* must it be presumed that his choice to transfer to a religious institute did not elicit their disapproval;

c) Nor could it be said that the financial assistance was so definitely and reservedly destined to one particular diocese that a cleric studying for another was absolutely excluded from sharing in its benefits. A diocesan seminarian aspiring to the religious life would similarly not be excluded from the share spent on his education, even though he were forced to leave his proper diocese to find the religious institute of his choice. Indeed, a group of regular clerics dispersed throughout various dioceses could be said to fulfill also the needs of a particular diocese from which a seminarian departed in the first place. One could regard as acting as a substitute in his place any religious community in the vicinity of the latter diocese, for quite readily the bishop could call upon its help. As a result, a certain kind of compensation would arise among various dioceses

[22] As given by Bouix, *De Jure Regularium,* I, 551.

and religious institutes, a compensation which should be considered as satisfying completely the intention of the donors. For as these same benefactors did not specifically determine their intention in setting up the fund, it should rightly be presumed as directed to the general good and benefit of souls. Hence in such an intention one could expect to find included the liberty of making profession in a religious institute.

To Bouix, these arguments of his contemporary seemed to have intrinsic value and be the result of logical reasoning.[23]

Of a slightly different opinion was Daris (1821-1905). Together with certain others whose names he did not mention, he agreed with the first opinion of Bouix, namely, that at least for a notable length of time priests who had been supported and trained from a seminary fund would be bound in fulfillment of what he called a tacit contract to serve in the sacred ministry in the diocese for which they were trained.[24]

Piatus said that if the benefactors had expressed service for a number of years in a definite diocese as a requisite for the use of the burse, then the cleric certainly would be obliged to conform to this obligation, unless his salvation were endangered by remaining in the world.[25] In the absence of a restriction of this kind, Piatus did not think that a cleric was bound, and for his conclusion he quoted an enactment (revoked by the Holy See) of a Synod of Cesena: "Ut si vel Religionem aliquam, aut Congregationem ingredi voluerint, vel ad statum laicalem redire, sumptus seminario refundant..."

[23] *De Jure Regularium,* I, 551-552.

[24] Joseph Daris, *Quaestiones canonico-civiles de Statu Religioso, Praelectiones Canonicae* (5 vols., Leodii: Verhoben-Debeur, 1863-1874), IV, p. 42, as cited by Piatus, *Praelectiones Iuris Regularis,* I, 77.

[25] *Praelectiones Iuris Regularis,* I, 77. Cf. Vermeersch, who practically held the same opinion.—*De Religiosis Institutis,* I, n. 135; Icard, *Praelectiones Juris Canonici habitae in seminario Sancti Sulpitii,* II, n. 459, p. 259.

The Sacred Congregation of the Council, on February 26, 1695, commanded that the prohibition against entrance into religion be omitted from this statute because in this case the student did not abandon the clerical state but rather attached himself to it by a stricter bond.[26]

Daris would also have extended this prohibition against entering religion to those clerics who, with a dispensation from the Holy See, had been ordained without a title of benefice or patrimony, because such dispensation was given on account of the needs of the diocese and, by accepting it, the candidates promised, at least tacitly, to serve a particular diocese under obedience to its bishop.[27] But Piatus mentioned that this assertion was merely gratuitous and that to argue against a known right on account of a weak presumption was bad logic.[28]

Vermeersch argued much the same as Piatus and added that, unless in the constitution of a burse it was explicitly stated that those clerics who have been trained and supported from it were bound by such a specific obligation, the question had to be settled according to the common liberty of clerics, in virtue of which entrance into the religious life was permitted.[29] Furthermore, a cleric during his time of studies was not strictly obliged to manifest either to his bishop or to the superiors of the seminary his intention to enter the religious life. He continued: "Nam haec est communis ex jure conditio alumnorum seminarii, ut publice instituantur; et tamen ex eodem jure integrum est clericis Religionem ingredi."[30]

An opposite opinion was held by Icard in regard to those who had been helped to ordination through diocesan support:

[26] *Praelectiones Iuris Regularis, loc. cit.* This decree of the Sacred Congregation is given by Franciscus Monacelli, *Formularii Legalis Practici fori Ecclesiastici Supplementum ad tom. II* (Venetiis, 1751), n. 108.

[27] *Ibid.*, p. 43.

[28] *Loc. cit.*

[29] *De Religiosis Institutis*, I, n. 135.

[30] Vermeersch, *loc. cit.*

> Id servitium dioecesis autem exigere potest Episcopus, etiamsi non intercesserit explicita promissio, ab iis generatim qui sumptibus dioecesis aliti sunt, ut ei operam suam praestent cujus beneficio ad dignitatem officii clericalis conscenderunt.[31]

In the rules of the seminary, Saint Charles Borromeo (1538-1584) had made a similar praescription:

> Si quis decursu temporis de statu mutando consilium caperet, etiamsi de religione ingredienda cogitaret, de eo R. Archiepiscopum vel rectorem certiorem faciat; peccaret enim si in seminario hoc animo viveret, in alium finem consumens quod ad operarios solum pro hujus Ecclesiae auxilio sustentando est constitutum.[32]

Article 3. The Promise of Obedience to the Bishop

Although clerics as a matter of general recognition possessed the liberty to seek admission into cloistered walls, yet there were times when the exercise of this freedom was not deemed opportune, according to Pope Benedict XIV. He said it would indeed be disagreeable and for an ecclesiastic, when he had promised reverence and obedience to his bishop at his ordination, to leave his diocese without the knowldege of his bishop and to bind himself pereptually to the service of a religious institute.

The Pope was eager to favor the correct and equitable doctrine concerning the reverence and obedience promised to the bishop. By way of example he referred to the oath of fidelity and obedience which Pope Innocent II (1198-1216) required: "Ego talis ab hac hora in antea fidelis ero, et obediens Placentinae Ecclesiae, et Domino meo Episcopo Placentino." Pope Benedict XIV explained that this oath was taken in favor of the Cathedral Chapter, to which the cleric was thenceforward obligated, but that principally the cleric was obligated to the bishop as its

[31] *Op. cit.*, II, n. 459, p. 260.

[32] *Institutiones seminarii*, pars III, c. 1, as cited in *Praelectiones Juris Canonici habitae in seminario Sancti Sulpitii, loc. cit.*

head.[33] The Pope insisted that he held in no less respect a solemn promise of this kind which according to a very ancient custom in the Church was undoubtedly in practice a thousand years before his time. He contended, therefore, that a priest, in virtue of such a promise, is prevented from leaving, except with the bishop's approval, the church for which he was ordained.[34] On this very same point, however, St. Alphonsus Liguori remarked that the Pope's statement did not refer to those clerics who intended to transfer to the religious life.[35] To strengthen his own position, as stated before, the Pope referred to Hallier († 1659), who with the best arguments refuted the stand of a French writer whose purpose it had been to belittle the true worth of this promised reverence and obedience.[36]

Notwithstanding his great respect for the cleric's promise to his bishop, Pope Benedict XIV still did not consider that the establishment of a general law in this regard was needed, for a) whatever need might arise, there would usually be sufficient provision for the case in existing ecclesiastical law, and b) if further legislation were needed, the matter could not be considered as requiring general legislation.[37]

Bouix held that the oath of obedience made to the bishop at the cleric's reception of sacred orders was pronounced according to the tenor of Church law, the canons of which reserved to clerics the right of entering religion whenever they so desired.[38]

Article 4. The Judgment of the Bishop

To the objection that a bishop had the better knowledge of his clerics, and that he, rather than anyone else, could

[33] C. 19, X, *de verborum significatione*, V, 40.

[34] Ep. *Ex quo*, §11.

[35] *Theologia Moralis*, lib. VI, tr. 5, n. 828.

[36] Franciscus Hallier, *de sacris electionibus et ordinationibus* (2. ed., 3 vols., Romae, 1740), tom. I, part. 1, sec. 6, §12; Ep. *Ex quo*, §11.

[37] Ep. *Ex quo*, §12.

[38] *De Jure Regularium*, I, 545.

judge whether entrance into the religious state was useful to the cleric himself and for the general benefit of the Church, Bouix answered that ordinarily a cleric did not disclose the secrets of his heart to the bishop, nor was he obliged to do so. Of great importance was it, however, that correct advice be extended the cleric in such matters. Bouix thought that a religious superior would be the more competent judge of a religious vocation because of his acquaintance with the novitiate requirements, and because he, rather than a bishop, would know thoroughly the qualifications demanded of a candidate in the particular religious institute. Then, again, a bishop would be accustomed, and rightly so, to treat with special consideration those of his clergy who excelled in piety and other qualities. Hence, continued Bouix, it was rightly presumed that he would allow their departure reluctantly. Through this it could happen on account of human frailty to which bishops are not immune, that dissensions would arise between the regulars and the diocesan prelate.[39] Hence, it was only prudent to have a canonical requirement which did not leave to the decision of the bishop the desirability of entrance into the religious life on the part of one of his clerics. It mattered little if this arrangement should seem inconvenient to some person. Whoever wished that the Church's allowance of clerics to enter the religious life be changed, and that the matter be left entirely in the hands of the bishop, should be very cautious lest he trust his own arguments too boldly, and consider himself wiser than the Fathers of the Church and the Church itself.[40]

ARTICLE 5. GRAVE HARM TO THE CHURCH AND THE CLERIC'S RECALL FROM A RELIGIOUS INSTITUTE

There was never any enactment of general legislation which would have authorized a bishop to recall under threat of penalty a cleric from the religious life for a resumption

[39] Bouix, *De Jure Regularium,* I, 545.
[40] *Ibid.,* p. 546.

of service in the diocese. Thomassinus († 1695) contended that a cleric, if filled with zeal for a holier and a more austere life, and if eagerly seeking admittance into a monastery, was not to be prevented from the fulfillment of his purpose, and much less was he to be withdrawn from the monastery in which he had been professed. This contention the author[41] based on the admonition of Pope Gregory the Great to Bishop Desiderius, who attempted the recall of one of his deacons. In this case the bishop was rather to encourage the cleric to a most constant perseverance in his flight from the cares and vanity of the world, from which clerics are not always disentangled.[42]

Fagnanus had held the opposite opinion:

> ... quia cum propter salutem animarum clericus possit a religione avocari, etiamsi cum licentia transierit ... multo fortius ex eadem causa hoc fieri poterit, quando transivit licentia Praelati non petita, vel etiam denegata.[43]

A more explicit presentation from authoritative sources of the mode of action to be followed when a cleric's abandoned church suffered serious harm was given by Pope Benedict XIV in his letter *Ex quo.* Just as in a particular case and for certain reasons a superior of a less strict Order was able to ask for the return of his regular subject who had transferred to a stricter Order even after his solemn profession in the latter monastery, so likewise a bishop could demand (*repetere possit*) in certain cases with just and urgent reasons the return of his clerical subject already admitted into an Order of regulars.[44] This principle

[41] L. Thomassinus, *Vetus et Nova Ecclesiae Disciplina circa Beneficia et Beneficiarios* (ed. postrema, Parisiis, 3 vols., Magontiaci, 1691), II, lib. 1, cap. 12, n. 18.

[42] *Supra*, p. 4.

[43] *Commentaria in Quinque Libros Decretalium,* III, c. 18, X, *de regularibus et transeuntibus ad religionem,* III, 31, n. 29.

[44] Ep. *Ex quo,* §18. In commenting on this principle, St. Alphonsus Liguori stressed the fact that, even should a cleric have pronounced solemn vows, the same would be true and therefore the cleric could be recalled.—*Theologia Moralis,* lib. VI, tr. 5, n. 828; Bouix, sub-

he based on the conclusion of Pope Innocent IV (1243-1254): "Crederemus tamen, quod posset eum repetere, si ex transitu sua prima Ecclesia gravem sustineret iacturam," and of Panormitanus, who commented on this same statement of Innocent IV: "... si Ecclesia graviter laederetur, esset revocandus."[45]

Concerning these statements, Pope Benedict XIV stated that sufficient provision had beeen made in the general law for a case in which a bishop wished to attack (*impugnare*) the fact of his cleric's departure to which he had been opposed. Consequently no new papal constitution was considered necessary to the end that episcopal rights might be asserted. The existing general rule the Pope thought sufficient for a prudent judge in individual cases.[46]

That the exercise of this right on the part of the bishop would not present little difficulty was acknowledged by the Pope. He mentioned that in regard to a beneficed cleric, a canon, and an archdeacon, the problem of ascertaining resultant harm to the church might not be serious; for instance, the office and dignity of an archdeacon, which in antiquity was of the utmost importance, was reduced to the role of a mere assistance to the bishop in general ordinations. On the other hand, in evaluating the need of pastors and other priests charged with the care of souls, the Pope asserted that they were of great importance to the Church. Yet it could not be denied that this office of spiritual leadership was less secure in respect to salvation than the state of religion.[47] As a result, any pastor desirous of embracing the religious life could in this one exception protect himself in court against his bishop (*in*

scribing to the same proposition, added that in practice, however, this grave harm would seldom be present, since the bishop could easily substitute another cleric to fill the vacant office or benefice of the departed cleric.—*De Jure Regularium,* I, 549.

[45] *Supra,* p. 14.

[46] Ep. *Ex quo,* §18.

[47] The Pope quoted Suarez speaking of the care of souls.—*Opera Omnia,* XV, lib. I, cap. 21, n. 5.

iudicio se tuebitur adversus Episcopum) who attempted to recall him to further service in the diocese. Pope Benedict XIV explained this one exception by referring to a letter of Pope Gregory the Great, who had rebuked the Emperor Mauritius (582-602) for prohibiting soldiers from admittance to the religious life. The exact quotation from Pope Gregory's letter is as follows:

> Multi sunt, qui possunt religiosam vitam etiam cum seculari habitu ducere, et plerique sunt, qui, nisi omnia reliquerint, salvari apud Deum nullatenus possunt.[48]

Therefore any beneficed cleric, canon, archdeacon, or pastor who had given up his work in the diocese for the sake of the religious life could affirm that he must be numbered not among the *multi,* but among the *plerique,* as indicated by Saint Gregory.[49]

To the objection that the clerical aspirant to the religious life had been doing great works of charity for the poor, the cleric could answer that with the required permission from his superior in the religious institute he could continue this noble work by means of the possessions he had brought with him. Pope Benedict XIV again referred to the same letter of Pope Gregory the Great wherein the latter rebuked the Emperor Mauritius for prohibiting persons in debt from entering religion.[50]

Again, if an objection were raised against the old age of a priest who wished to transfer to a religious institute, Pope Benedict XIV asserted that to this an answer was easy and obvious, for there were many religious men who having grown old were still doing laudable work according to their various talents.[51]

[48] Lib. II, ep. 62—Mansi, IX, 1152; Ep. *Ex quo,* §19.

[49] Ep. *Ex quo,* §19. Cf. Piatus, *Praelectiones Iuris Regularis,* I, 78; Vermeersch, *De Religiosis Institutis,* I, n. 136.

[50] Lib. II, ep. 62—Mansi, IX, 1152; Ep. *Ex quo,* §20.

[51] Lib. II, ep. 62—Mansi, IX, 1152; Ep. *Ex quo,* §§20, 21.

PART TWO

CANONICAL COMMENTARY

CHAPTER VI

THE APPLICATION OF THE IMPEDIMENT AS TO CLERICS

ARTICLE 1. CLERICS IN SPECIAL CASES AND THE EFFECT OF THE IMPEDIMENT UPON THEM

> **Canon 542, 2°: Illicite, sed valide admittuntur: *Clerici in sacris constituti,* inconsulto loci Ordinario aut eodem contradicente ex eo quod eorum discessus in grave animarum detrimentum cedat, quod aliter vitari minime possit (italics added).**

From the wording of the canon it is quite evident that the impediment does not apply to clerics who have received only minor orders, namely the orders of an acolyte, an exorcist, a lector or a porter[1] or to a cleric who has received first tonsure only.[2] Furthermore, it grants the minor clerics an implicit permission to enter the religious life, although they have not consulted their ordinary. If the law allows them to return to the lay state,[3] then so much the more are they to be permitted to enter the religious state. Natural equity[4] and the special reverence and submission which clerics owe to their ordinary would demand of them that they notify their ecclesiastical superior of their plan to embrace the religious life.[5] Moreover, the aforementioned impediment does not affect seminarians who have not received major orders. Neither does it apply to these same seminarians even when they have been supported and edu-

[1] Cf. can. 949: "In canonibus ... nomine ordinum *maiorum* vel *sacrorum* intelliguntur presbyteratus, diaconatus, subdiaconatus; *minorum* vero acolythatus, exorcistatus, lectoratus, ostiariatus;"

[2] Cf. can. 950 and can. 542, 2°.

[3] Cf. can. 211, §2.

[4] Timotheus Schaefer, *De Religiosis ad Normam Codicis Iuris Canonici* (4. ed., Typis Polyglottis Vaticanis: Roma, 1947), p. 441, n. 803 (hereafter cited as *De Religiosis*).

[5] Franciscus Wernz et Petrus Vidal, *Ius Canonicum* (7 vols. in 8, Romae: Universitas Gregoriana, 1923-1938 [Vols. II et V, 3. ed., 1943 et 1946; Vol. VI, 2. ed., 1949]), III, 207.

cated from a diocesan fund for future service in a given diocese.[6]

Does the extent of this impediment include clerics who are under an obligation towards their bishop or their diocese by reason of an oath or a promise? The question is asked in regard to the following obligations: a) the oath demanded for promotion to orders on the part of a candidate who has a present domicile in a diocese different from that of his place of origin; b) the oath required of a cleric who is formally excardinated and pledges perpetual service to the new diocese; c) the oath exacted of a candidate for major orders who is to be ordained under the title of "service of the diocese" and consists in his sworn promise to devote himself perpetually to the service of the diocese in which he is already incardinated;[7] d) the promise of reverence and obedience to the proper ordinary, as required in the ordination ceremony.

A. Clerics Subject to the Oath of Canon 956

> . . . aut simplex domicilium sine origine; sed in hoc altero casu promovendus debet animum in dioecesi perpetuo manendi iureiurando firmare, . . .

The oath of canon 956 is taken by a layman desirous of being included among the clergy of a diocese other than

[6]Such gratuitous support and education is sometimes given to a diocesan seminarian who cannot afford to pay any of the expenses involved. This presents a problem later, when this seminarian intends to follow a religious vocation. The difficulty is precisely whether or not the failure of making repayment to the diocesan seminary causes grave harm to souls, so that the bishop may canonically impede the seminarian's entry to religion, especially after the reception of a major order. It will be discussed in Chapter VII, Art. 4, B.

[7] This oath is analogous to the one prescribed by the same canon (981) by which a candidate for major orders is ordained under the "title of the mission" in places subject to the jurisdiction of the Sacred Congregation for the Propagation of the Faith. By this oath the candidate promises to give himself perpetually to the service of the diocese of the specified mission to which he is to be sent.

the one that juridically marks his place of origin. This sworn statement guarantees his intention of establishing a domicile in the new diocese. This is required of him for the purpose of obtaining a proper bishop for his promotion to the clerical state. Hence, it must be made sometime before the actual reception of tonsure. It must be borne in mind that this oath does not refer to the service of the diocese, but rather simply qualifies or fortifies the election of a domicile. It adds a great act of religion to the formal element required for the acquisition of a domicile for any purpose as delineateed in canon 92, §1. But the latter canon admits the contingency expressed in the clause, *si nihil inde avocet,* and hence the oath of canon 956 contains it too. The mere foreseeing of contingencies which might cause him to withdraw from that domicile before the reception of tonsure would not nullify his oath any more than it would his initial intention. If during the interval extending from the pronouncing of the oath to the reception of tonsure the candidate should decide to enter a religious institute, he would be entirely free to do so, despite the oath. Once tonsure is received, he becomes subject to the bishop by a new tie;[8] the final purpose of the oath has been attained. Much less would the cleric in regard to entering religion be bound by this oath after the reception of tonsure. Therefore,. it can rightly be said that the declaratory[9] oath of canon 956, necessary in some cases for the obtaining of a proper bishop for ordination, does not add to or substract from the canonical effects of canon 542, 2° *pr.* It does not increase the bishop's power of impeding entrance into religion, since it does not extend the force of the impediment. Such an oath is part of the common legislation of the Code, and it is only logical to conclude that it is not an exception overlooked in the

[8] James T. McBride, *Incardination and Excardination of Seculars,* The Catholic University of America Canon Law Studies, n. 145 (Washington, D.C.: The Catholic University of America Press, 1941), pp. 333-334.

[9] McBride, *op. cit.,* p. 551.

formulation of the impediment. Certainly the oath does not decrease the freedom of clerics to embrace the religious life. It is included in the extent of the impediment of canon 542, 2° *pr.*, and does not alter the application of the same impediment.

B. Clerics Bound by the Oath of Canon 117, 3°

> **Ad incardinationem alieni clerici Ordinarius ne deveniat, nisi clericus iureiurando coram eodem Ordinario eiusve delegato declaraverit se in perpetuum novae dioecesis servitio velle addici ad normam sacrorum canonum.**

Whenever a cleric is to be canonically transferred to another diocese through excardination and incardination, the second ordinary (*ad quem*) may not lawfully proceed to the actual incardination, unless the cleric has declared by oath before him or his delegate that he wishes to be attached in perpetuity to the service of the second diocese, according to the norms of canon law. While the oath for acquiring a domicile for ordination according to canon 956 must be taken before ordination, this oath for excardination must be taken in every instance, even by priests. It is a sworn assertion of the cleric's actual intention of perpetually binding himself to the service of the new diocese. Yet it is not a promissory oath. Consequently it does not effect that a newly incardinated cleric is bound to the diocese with any stronger ties than are those who are ordained for its service while having their original domicile in it. A cleric, therefore, who has taken this oath may still be excardinated from the diocese or also enter religion at some later time.[10] This oath does not change the canonical force of the impediment of canon 542, 2° *pr.* The only two restrictions of 542, 2° *pr.* upon the liberty of clerics in major orders, forming as they do the basic foundation of the impediment, remain the same regardless of this oath.

[10] Cf. Ioanne Chelodi, *Ius Canonicum de Personis* (3. ed., Trento, 1942), p. 177, n. 107; McBride, *op cit.*, pp. 548-549.

C. Clerics Subject to the Oath of Canon 981

I. The Canonical Force of the Oath Itself

> ... suppleri potest titulo servitii dioecesis ... ita tamen ut ordinatus, iureiurando interposito, se devoveat perpetuo dioecesis ... servitio ...

Candidates who are promoted to major orders under this supplementary title of "service to the diocese," must before their ordination take the oath to serve the diocese permanently. The force of this oath, a promissory one, is that it specifies the already existing obligation of canonical obedience of canon 128, which states that any office assigned to clerics by the ordinary must be accepted and faithfully performed as often and as long as the bishop judges that the needs of the Church demand it, unless a legitimate impediment excuses them. The obligation of this canon, therefore, is confirmed by the virtue of religion,[11] and lasts as long as the cleric does not legitimately change this title under which he was ordained.[12] Moreover, this promissory oath "partakes of the nature and conditions of the act promised by oath. If an act which involves directly the injury of others, or prejudices the common weal or one's eternal salvation, is confirmed by an oath, the act does not thereby acquire any justification."[13] Consequently, the obligation assumed through a promissory oath ceases if the object promised by means of an oath becomes an obstacle to a higher good.[14] But the act by which a cleric binds

[11] Udalricus Beste, *Introductio in Codicem* (3. ed., Collegeville: St. John's Abbey Press, 1946), ad can. 981 (hereafter cited as Beste).

[12] Anonymous, "De Clericorum Ingressu in Religionem," *Periodica de Religiosis et Missionariis*, Brugis, 1905-1919; from 1920: *Periodica de Re Canonica et Morali utilia praesertim Religiosis et Missionariis*, Brugis, 1920-1927; from 1927: *Periodica de Re Morali, Canonica, Liturgica*, Brugis (1927-1936) et Romae (1937—), XIII (1924-1925), 215 (hereafter cited as *Periodica*).

[13] Can. 1318, §§1 and 2. The translation is taken from Stanislaus Woywod, *A Practical Commentary on the Code* (revised ed., 2 vols., New York: Joseph F. Wagner, Inc., 1948), II, 104 (hereafter cited as Woywod).

[14] Can. 1319, §2.

himself to the service of the diocese includes the contingency of entry into religion. This conclusion is based on a dictum of Gratian in his Decree,[15] on the opinion of St. Thomas Aquinas[16] and on the authority of Pope Benedict XIV.[17] The force of this promissory oath, therefore, ceases by the very fact that it impedes the way to a greater good. In no way does the perpetuity of this oath promising service to the diocese impede licit entrance into religion.[18] This oath does not expand the orbit of the impediment against clerics in major orders who desire to embrace the religious life.

II. The Oath and Its Relation to Canon 542, 1° *ult.*

It might be argued that the oath of canon 981 gives rise, indirectly at least, to an impediment against entry into religion by clerics in major orders, i.e., that the oath of "service of the diocese" is identical with, or included in, the one demanded by the Holy See in special cases (*ex instituto S. Sedis*).[19] Concerning the possible connection between the oath of canon 981 and the impediment of canon 542, 1° *ult.*, a writer in the *Periodica*[20] presents intrinsic

[15] Ad c. 1, C. XIX, q. 2.

[16] *Summa Theologica,* IIa-IIae, q. 189, a. 7.

[17] Ep. *Ex quo,* §§6 and 7.

[18] G. Arendt, "De Can. 542 et 981," *Jus Pontificium* (Romae, 1921-1940), IV (1924), 184 (hereafter cited as *Jus Pont.*).

[19] Can. 542, 1° *ult.* "Invalide ad novitiatum admittuntur: Clerici qui ex instituto Sanctae Sedis iureiurando tenentur operam suam navare in bonum suae dioecesis vel missionum, pro eo tempore quo iurisiurandi obligatio perdurat."

[20] *Periodica,* XIII (1924-1925), 145-148. The writer referred to is either Vermeersch or Creusen, for in his article he makes reference to "nostrâ Epitome iuris c., I, 534, pr. ed." of which the authors are Vermeersch-Creusen. The appearance of this article was founded on a tenuous supposition, i.e., that the writer in *Il Monitore Ecclesiastico* (Romae, 1876—), Serie IV, Vol. V, Fasc. X (Ottobre 1924), p. 311, held an opinion which in reality he did not hold. The background of the discussion is as follows: *Il Monitore Ecclesiastico* was asked whether or not it may be demanded in synodal statutes that seminarians who had received a gratuitous seminary education be obliged to

arguments to show that the two canons are entirely unrelated and independent of each other. As the present writer considers them to be the result of sound, canonically correct reasoning, they will be summarized here. His arguments are based on:

a) The words of the Code. The Code itself states that only such clerics are forbidden to enter religion who are bound by a vow *ex instituto S. Sedis.* But evidently such an oath established by the Holy See refers to a singular instance in law and not to the common law of the Church. Certainly the common law is never referred to, in juridical language, as resulting *ex instituto S. Sedis.* Moreover, the oath of canon 542, 1° *ult.* places its prohibition against entrance into the novitiate only for the time that is specified in the oath. It is, therefore, temporary. As the oath of canon 981 does not include any time limit, it must be concluded that it would be a perpetual impediment, if any at

take an oath forbidding them to enter religion within the time of seven years after their ordination. The questioner had expressed his doubt that such legislation was in agreement with the discipline of the Code. To this request *Il Monitore Ecclesiastico* replied that such an oath is entirely superfluous in view of canons 542 and 981. Canon 981, the respondent continued, prescribes an oath by which a cleric binds himself perpetually to the service of his diocese. Hence not even upon the lapse of seven years might a cleric licitly enter the religious life without his bishop's release, which of course could not be demanded. The priest had freely placed this perpetual bond upon himself. In the absence of the oath of canon 981, the respondent added, a major cleric is still bound by the impediment of canon 542, 2° *pr.* The same writer in *Il Monitore Ecclesiastico* continued along a similar trend, nowhere saying that the oath of canon 981 is included in the one *ex instituto S. Sedis,* which of course is canonically correct. And therefore the respondent seemed to have a reasonable cause for complaint when later he was accused of having expressed such an erronous opinion. His complaint and his own defense appeared in a second article in *Il Monitore Ecclesiastico,* Serie IV, Vol. V, Fasc. XII (Dicembre 1924), 367-368. In answer to this second article there appeared another article in the *Periodica, XIII* (1924-1925), 213-215, wherein the writer admits his fault, but expresses his disagreement with the importance placed upon the oath of canon 981 as a prohibition against licit entrance into religion.

all. Hence the two canons must be considered quite distinct from each other.

b) The practice (*stylus*) of the Code. The codifiers of the Code of Canon Law, in order to avoid conflicting legislation, are careful to preserve the contents of one canon by inserting in another canon a phrase similar to this: *firmo tamen tali canone.* Yet in the canons treating of admission into religion, no such redeeming clause can be found for canon 981, which would be necessary if it were to evince an additional impediment.

c) The absurdity of any opposite conclusion. An absurd conclusion would be arrived at if canon 981 were included in canon 542, 1° *ult.*, because, if this were true, then a pastor ordained under the canonical title of benefice[21] would be bound only by the impediment of canon 542, 2° *pr.*, while a pastor who had been ordained under the title of "service of the diocese" would be bound by that same impediment in addition to the one of canon 542, 1° *ult.*

d) The permissible change of the title of ordination. The oath of canon 981 cannot be said to possess a binding force for a longer time than the duration of the title itself with which it is connected. But there is no law forbidding such a change of title of "service of the diocese." The service to the diocese in perpetuity is promised only to compensate for the perpetual support acquired by the cleric in sacred orders.

e) A comparison of the oath-formulae. In the oath *ex instituto S. Sedis* there is found an express mention of the fact that thereby the cleric will faithfully serve the diocese or mission to the exclusion of entering religion unless permission from the Holy See has been obtained.[22] Yet in the oath of "service of the diocese" there does not

[21] Can. 979.

[22] "Ego ... spondeo et iuro quod, postquam ad sacros ordines promotus fuero, nullam religionem, Societatem aut Congregationem regularem, sine speciali Sedi Apostolicae licentia ... ingrediar neque in earum aliquam professionem emittam."—*Collectanea S. C. P. F.*, II, n. 1369, *in fine.*

occur any mention excluding future entrance into religion. Again, in the oath *ex instituto S. Sedis,* the disallowance of entry to religion is modified in so far as special permission can be obtained from the Holy See.[23] The oath of perpetual service to the diocese contains no such qualifying phrase. To suppose that the Roman Pontiff forbids more strictly the entry into religion through the oath of "service to the diocese" than through the oath *ex instituto S. Sedis* can hardly be sustained. Yet this is the obvious but absurd conclusion to which one is forced, since the law itself makes provisions for the obtaining of special permission to enter religion in the one oath, but contains no such provision in the other case.

In addition to the intrinsic arguments, the writer in the *Periodica*[24] produces extrinsic arguments founded on the opinion of many authors, among whom are such noted canonists as Blat,[25] Prümmer,[26] Cocchi[27] and Bouuaert-Simenon.[28] They agreed that the oath of canon 542, 1° *ult.* refers only to the seminarians educated at the College of the Sacred Congregation for the Propagation of the Faith and in other Roman colleges. They likewise maintain, at least implicitly, that this oath is entirely separate from that of canon 981.

Typical of their statements is the one expressed by Bouuaert-Simenon in writing about the oath *ex instituto S. Sedis*:

[23] To this special permission, an explicit reference is made in the oath-formula given in the previous footnote.

[24] *Ibid.*, pp. 148-150.

[25] Albertus Blat, *Commentarium Textus Codicis Iuris Canonici* (6 vols., Romae, 1919-1927), II, *De Personis*, n. 610, p. 596 (hereafter cited as *Commentarium Textus Codicis*).

[26] Dominicus Prümmer, *Manuale Iuris Canonici* (3. ed., 2 vols., Friburgi Brisgoviae, 1922), q. 204, n. 8 (hereafter cited as Prümmer).

[27] Guidus Cocchi, *Commentarium in Codicem Iuris Canonici*, Vol. IV (3. ed., Taurinorum Augustae, 1932), Lib. II, Pars II, *De Religiosis*, n. 64, p. 136.

[28] F. Claeys Bouuaert et G. Simenon, *Manuale Juris Canonici*, Vol. I (5. ed., Gandae et Leodii: Apud Auctores, 1939), n. 640.

> Hoc institutum exsistit in collegio S.C.P.F. et aliis pluribus collegiis Urbis. Eodem impedimento non ligantur clerici qui ad norman c. 981, titulo *missionis* vel *servitii dioecesis* ordinati sunt.[29]

Hence it is concluded that the oath of canon 981 does not constitute an additional impediment against clerics in major orders. And a major cleric under such oath is held by the same two restrictions outlined in canon 542, 2° *pr.* as is any other cleric ordained under a title not requiring this oath.

D. Clerics Bound by the Promise of Reverence and Obedience as Required in the Ordination Ceremony

In the rite of ordination to the priesthood the Roman Pontifical prescribes that the cleric again approach the ordaining bishop and, on bended knees, place his joined hands between those of the bishop who asks: "Do you promise reverence and obedience to me and my successors?" The cleric answers, "I promise." If the cleric's ordinary is different from the ordaining bishop, he promises this same reverence and obedience to his proper bishop, but through the ordaining bishop.[30]

Some authors held that this promise binds a secular priest gravely, through the virtue of fidelity, to show special reverence and obedience to the bishop, even in such a manner that the cleric is forbidden to leave the diocese without his bishop's permission.[31] Others hold that this obligation of fidelity arising from the promise is light (*levem esse*), while still others maintain that no particular obligation of reverence and obedience, distinct from that which any major cleric owes his proper ordinary, arises from this promise.[32]

[29] *Loc. cit.*

[30] *Pontificale Romanum* (3 parts in 1 vol., Mechliniae: H. Dessain, 1895), tit. *de ordinatione presbyteri,* p. 282.

[31] Cf. Franciscus Hallier, *De sacris electionibus et ordinationibus,* I, part. I, sect. 6, §12.

[32] Cf. F. Cappello, *Tractatus Canonico-Moralis de Sacramentis,* Vol. IV (2. ed., Augustae Taurinorum, Romae, 1947), pp. 472-473, n. 656.

To Cappello it seems that this declaration of fidelity to one's ordinary is a promise in the true and proper sense, and that from this promise there necessarily arises an obligation. As it is a special kind of promise, he continues, it also sets up a special indebtedness to show reverence and obedience to one's ordinary. Yet Cappello does not hold that the obligation of fidelity arising from this promise is a grave one,[33] while on the other hand he does oblige the cleric, in virtue of this promise, to respect and obey his ordinary as demanded in the canons, and does not permit the cleric to leave the service of his diocese.[34]

Nevertheless this promise and subsequent indebtedness to his ordinary neither prohibits a cleric from entry to religion, nor does it broaden the extent of the impediment of canon 542, 2° *pr.* As long as the priest consults his proper ordinary and is not opposed by him on the ground that grave harm will come to souls by his departure, he can feel assured that this promise of reverence made to his bishop at ordination does not bring about an impediment precluding entry into religion. The same can also be said of the three other oaths discussed under this article. The provisions requiring the oaths and the resulting certainty of the promise strengthened by them are part of the common law of the Church. But in legislating for the admission into the novitiate of clerics in major orders, the Code makes no reference or distinction in regard to these oaths. Consequently, it is logical to conclude that they were not meant to be restrictions additional to the two found in the first of the listed impediments that preclude licit admission into the novitiate.

Article 2. Clerics Affected by the Impediments

While the impediments against licit admission into the

[33] ". . . dicenda videntur: Huius obligatio fidelitatis, *quatenus oritur ex praefata promissione*, non urget sub gravi: certo sane non constat de eiusdem gravitate, ideoque mitius diudicandum."—Cappello, *op. cit.*, p. 473, n. 657.

[34] *Loc. cit.;* cf. canons 111, 117, 127, 128, 143, 144.

novitiate does not apply to clerics in minor orders, it does include the clerics ordained to major orders. Canon 542, 2° *pr.*, it is true, does not specify who are meant by the term, *clerici in sacris constituti*, but there is a later canon, 949, under the title *De Ordine* in the third book of the Code, which states that, in canons pertinent to orders, by the terms "sacred or major orders" are understood the priesthood, diaconate and subdiaconate.[35] It includes, therefore, all priests, deacons, and subdeacons who have not consulted their local ordinary or who are opposed by him on the ground that their departure will cause grave harm to souls which cannot at all be avoided by other arrangements. It extends to all priests regardless of whatever rank of honor or position they occupy to the exclusion, however, of bishops at least preconized. The latter as well as titular and residential bishops are bound by a different impediment, one which invalidates their entrance into religion.[36]

The absence of the oath of "service to the diocese" demanded of clerics in major orders does not call for a milder application of the canonical impediment. Neither does the fact that some major clerics are not engaged in the actual care of souls or do not have a residential benefice influence the application of the impediment in their special circumstances. Concerning such clerics, however, it would be more difficult to allege grave harm to souls, which reason is the only one that entitles a local ordinary to oppose entry into religion by one of his subjects in major orders. On the other hand, in the case wherein clerics have received the charge of souls or are in possession of a residential benefice, the fact of serious injury to souls could be more easily verified.[37]

[35] "In canonibus qui sequuntur, nomine ordinum *maiorum vel sacrorum* intelliguntur presbyteratus, diaconatus, subdiaconatus; *minorum* vero acolythatus, exorcistatus, lectoratus, ostiariatus."

[36] Can. 542, 1°: "Invalide ad novitiatum admittuntur: Episcopus sive residentialis sive titularis, licet a Romano Pontifice sit tantum designatus."

[37] Cf. canons 143, 425, §1, 465, 440, 471, §4, 474, 448, §2, 2381.

Article 3. The Relationship Between the Impediment and the Reduction to the Lay State

What is the relationship between the impediment of canon 542, 2° *pr.* and the cleric who upon receiving major orders has subsequently become reduced to the lay state? Are such clerics, nevertheless, sufficiently established in holy orders (*constituti in sacris*) to be held by the restrictions of this impediment? The case can easily be envisioned in which a reduced cleric, because of his intimacy with things religious and holy, as also in consequence of his profound, spiritual convictions acquired during his seminary training, desires to renounce completely the world and its pleasures and to consecrate his entire self through public vows to the love and service to God. To establish the case more graphically, regard, for instance, the condition of a subdeacon who for reasons known to himself alone refuses to advance to higher orders; or his bishop cannot attain moral certitude concerning his canonical fitness and worthiness. In both instances the bishop is not to proceed with the ordination.[38]

According to an Instruction of the Sacred Congregation of the Sacraments,[39] the local ordinary, when knowing for certain, either from the candidate's declarations or from other sources, that he really has no vocation, shall have recourse to the Holy See, fully explaining the situation and giving the reasons for his grave doubt regarding the vocation and moral fitness to bear worthily and faithfully even greater burdens. In such an event the cleric may petition with the approval of the ordinary for a canonical reduction to the state of the laity. Whereupon the Holy See, considering the great obligations of a cleric in major orders and its solicitude for the welfare of souls, will probably

[38] Cf. can. 973, §§2 and 3.

[39] S. C. de Sacr., *Instructio ad Rmos locorum Ordinarios de scrutinio alumnorum peragendo antequam ad ordines promoveantur*, 27 dec. 1930, §3, n. 3—*Acta Apostolicae Sedis, Commentarium Officiale* (Romae, 1909-1929; Civitate Vaticana, 1929—), XXIII (1931), 126 (hereafter cited as *AAS*).

grant in a rescript the reduction to the lay state along with a dispensation from all the obligations including celibacy and the divine office.[40] After the subdeacon has received this rescript, may he licitly enter the novitiate for the brotherhood without previously consulting his local ordinary?

Canon 211 determines that sacred ordination once validly received cannot be invalidated, but that a cleric in major orders may be reduced to the state of the laity by rescript of the Holy See, by decree or sentence of the ecclesiastical court in the case mentioned in canon 214, or by the penalty of degradation. To appreciate more clearly the aforementioned difficulty, it will be necessary to consider briefly the nature of reduction to the lay state and its canonical effects.

A. The Nature of Reduction to the Lay State

A reduction to the lay state must be understood in its proper sense as an external, juridical or canonical reduction, one that leaves untouched the power of orders while it renders their use or exercise unlawful. There does not exist in the Church a theological or intrinsic reduction of clerics to the lay state such as would involve the loss of the sacramental character with its inherent power of orders and which as a result would make the acts of orders invalid. Certainly there is no intrinsic reduction in regard to orders which are of divine law, namely, the episcopate, the priesthood and the diaconate,[41] as their power is constituted by divine law and is dependent upon the indelible character impressed on the soul of the cleric. Consequently, a cleric who has received a hierarchical order cannot be truly and

[40] Cappello, *op. cit.*, p. 274, n. 381; cf. Francis P. Sweeney, *The Reduction of Clerics to the Lay State*, The Catholic University of America Canon Law Studies, n. 223 (Washington, D. C.: The Catholic University of America Press, 1945), pp. 124-125.

[41] Conc. Trident., sess. XXIII, *de ordine*, c. 1, can. 3-6—H. J. Schroeder, *Canons and Decrees of the Council of Trent* (St. Louis, Mo.: Herder, 1941), pp. 160 and 163.

internally expelled from the clerical state and reduced to the lay state.[42]

Since it is disputed among theologians and canonists whether the orders below the diaconate are merely of ecclesiastical institution or of divine origin, the Roman Pontiffs in practice never employ the power of rescinding these orders because of the danger of violating the divine law.[43] It is quite evident therefore that whoever has been enrolled in the clerical state, even through the reception of a minor order, is never again reduced, by an absolute and internal withdrawal of the order, to that state of the laity in which he was before ordination.

Although the Church declares that sacred ordination once validly received is never invalidated,[44] it does recognize and employ a juridical or external reduction to the lay state, which deprives the cleric of the rights, privileges and juridical status of clerics and renders him equal to a layman.[45] The Church can authorize such an extrinsic re-

[42] Cf. P. Gasparri, *Tractatus Canonicus de sacra ordinatione* (2 vols., Parisiis: Delhomme et Briguet, 1893), II, p. 294, n. 1142.

[43] Cf. S. Goyeneche, *Iuris Canonici Summa Principia*, Vol. I (Romae: Typis Polyglottis, 1935), 221.

[44] Cf. canons 211, § 1 and 950.

[45] Can. 213, § 1: Omnes qui e clericali statu ad laicalem legitime redacti aut regressi sunt, eo ipso amittunt officia, beneficia, iura ac privilegia clericalia et vetantur in habitu ecclesiastico incedere ac tonsuram deferre.

§2. Clericus tamen maior obligatione coelibatus tenetur, salvo praescripto, can. 214.

Although canon 213 speaks of those who are *reduced* or who *return* to the lay state, in the practical order the distinction does not imply any difference. The terminology of the Code itself does not indicate any marked distinction. In canon 211, §1, mention is made of the various methods by which a major cleric is reduced to the lay state. Yet canon 212, §2, refers to any major cleric who has returned to the lay state. Thus it appears that the canon refers to any major cleric who in any manner has been reduced or who has returned to the lay state.

Again, canon 211, §2, states that minor clerics return to the lay state through the way specified in the law. Among these methods are the dismissal of a minor religious cleric in temporary vows (can. 648)

duction, since the licit exercise of the power of orders, even those of divine origin, as well as the enjoyment of the rights and privileges of the clerical state is subject to the control of ecclesiastical jurisdiction.[46]

B. The Effects of Reduction to the Lay State

The juridical consequences resulting from a reduction to the lay state can be found in a comparison of those canons which grant certain rights and privileges with other canons which deprive the clergy of these same rights and privileges. Canon 118 declares that only clerics can obtain the power either of orders or of ecclesiastical jurisdiction, and ecclesiastical benefices and pensions. This legislation is in harmony with canon 213 which specifies, in regard to clerics who have been reduced to the lay state, the consequent effects of the loss of offices, benefices, rights and privileges of the clergy. Therefore together with the loss of the clerical state, these concomitant legal grants and effects likewise are taken from the cleric.

Canon 123 states that clerics cannot renounce the clerical privileges, i.e., the *privilegia canonis,*[47] *fori,*[84] *immunitatis,*[49] *et competentiae,*[50] but that he loses them when he is reduced to the lay state or is punished with the perpetual deprivation of the ecclesiastical garb. But when the penalty is remitted, or when he is again received into the ranks of the clergy, the privileges are recovered. Again, the pos-

and the dismissal of a minor religious cleric in perpetual vows (can. 669, §2). The canons themselves state, in both instances, that the cleric is reduced to the lay state. Consequently, there does not appear to be any need to search for a subtle distinction in the law.—*Sweeney, op. cit.* p. 166.

[46] Cf. Franciscus X. Wernz, *Ius Decretalium,* Vol. II, Pars 1, (3. ed., Prati, 1915), n. 229, p. 348; Stephen W. Findlay, *Canonical Norms Governing the Deposition and Degradation of Clerics,* The Catholic University of America Canon Law Studies, n. 130 (Washington, D. C.: The Catholic University of America Press, 1941), pp. 206-208 (hereafter cited as Findlay).

[47] Cf. can. 119.

[48] Cf. can. 120.

[49] Cf. can. 121.

[50] Cf. can. 122.

session or the lack of these clerical privileges depends upon the possession or the loss of the clerical state.

Canon 683 declares that it is not lawful for laymen to wear the clerical garb, with a few carefully defined exceptions. Upon the loss of the clerical state, this privilege of wearing the cassock is also taken away, according to the ruling of canon 213. This fact, too, makes manifest the canonical importance of the external, juridic state of a cleric if he is to have any rights and privileges. Although a cleric reduced to the lay state still possesses intrinsically in his soul the orders he has received, yet this is not sufficient to allow one to consider him in law a person able and capable to partake of the clerical rights and privileges.

Even the obligations imposed upon clerics depend, for the most part, on the fact that the cleric has not been reduced to the lay state. The third title of the second book of the Code expressly enumerates these obligations under canons 124-144. Beste[51] conveniently classifies them into positive and negative obligations. Among the positive obligations he lists piety,[52] obedience,[53] learning,[54] chastity,[55] the recitation of the divine office,[56] and the wearing of the ecclesiastical garb of tonsure;[57] among the negative obligations he records forbidden assumption of the risks of a surety,[58] unbecoming occupations and amusements,[59] military service,[60] business and trade,[61] and illegitimate absence.[62] Canon 213, §1, in treating of the effects of reduction to the lay state, does not mention anything at all about a suspension of the obligations as accompanying the clerical state. It is the observation of Blat,[63] however, that this release from the obligations is at least implicit, since in §2 of the same canon celibacy is the only obligation ex-

[51] *Op. cit.*, p. 181.

[52] Canons 125, 126.

[53] Canons 127, 128.

[54] Canons 129-131.

[55] Canons 132-134.

[56] Can. 135.

[57] Can. 136.

[58] Can. 137.

[59] Canons 138-140.

[60] Can. 141.

[61] Can. 142.

[62] Canons 143, 144.

[63] *Commentarium Textus Codicis*, II, *De Personis*, p. 188, n. 165.

pressly referred to as remaining the duty of a cleric in major orders reduced to the lay state. With this opinion the writer agrees, and he adds another reason by pointing to the explicit exclusion of the breviary obligation for reduced clerics in canon 135.

Sweeny,[64] in writing on *The Reduction of Clerics to the Lay State* and referring to the cessation of the clerical obligations, states it simply: "Since in the eyes of the Church and for legal effects a cleric who has been reduced to the lay state is a layman, it follows that such a cleric is no longer bound by the clerical obligations enumerated in canons 124-144." He cites Chelodi (1880-1822)[65] and Wernz (1842-1914)-Vidal (1867-1938)[66] as supporting his opinion. To these may be added Berutti,[67] Blat,[68] Bouscaren-Ellis[69] and Vermeersch-Creusen.[70] None of these authors offers any specific reasons for his stand. Among authors consulted, there was found no one to hold the opposite opinion,

[64] *Op. cit.*, p. 167.

[65] Ioannes Chelodi, *Ius de Personis iuxta Codicem Iuris Canonici* (2. ed., Tridenti: Libr. Edit. Tridentum, 1927), n. 124.

[66] *Ius Canonicum,* II, n. 395.

[67] Christophorus Berutti, *Institutiones Iuris Canonici,* Vol. II, Pars I (Taurini-Romae: Marietti, 1943), p. 134, n. 122 (hereafter cited as Berutti).

[68] *Commentarium Textus Codicis,* II, *De Personis,* p. 188, n. 165.

[69] Lincoln Bouscaren and Adam Ellis, *Canon Law, A Text and Commentary* (Bruce: Milwaukee, copyright 1946), p. 148 (hereafter cited as Bouscaren-Ellis). They point out that a major cleric who has suffered degradation remains bound not only to celibacy, but also to the recitation of the breviary, unless expressly exempted therefrom.—*Loc. cit.* By canon 213, §2, a major cleric who has been reduced to the lay state is bound to observe celibacy, except in the case noted in the provision outlined in canon 214.

[70] A. Vermeersch and I. Creusen, *Epitome Iuris Canonici,* Vol. I (7. ed., Mechliniae: Romae, H. Dessain, 1949), p. 282, n. 327 (hereafter cited as *Epitome*); concerning the effects upon the obligations of a cleric reduced to a lay state, Vermeersch-Creusen say: "... cessant obligationes status clericalis quae cum nova conditione non sunt compatibiles, nisi ex rescripto aut decreto plura definiantur. Clerico redacto ad statum laicalem licet militiam saecularem capessere, aliaque munera quaelibet honesta obire, a quibus soli clerici prohibentur."—*Loc. cit.*

while some omitted completely any reference to the obligations except the one referred to in the Code itself, i.e., that of celibacy.

In the light not only of the juridic importance of the clerical state for the possession of its accompanying rights, privileges and obligations, but also of the immediate loss of the concomitant rights, privileges and obligations upon the extrinsic reduction to the lay state, it must be concluded that the Church attaches a considerable significance and consequence to that action. Since authors are agreed in this that the clerical obligations which are officially mentioned under a separate title in the Code in canons 124-144 no longer bind after reduction to the lay state, it does not appear illogical, in fact it seems even more reasonable, to conclude that another obligation mentioned less formally elsewhere, i.e., that of canon 542, 2° *pr.* should likewise lose its binding force. Hardly is it forcing the concept of obligation to apply that idea to a major cleric's duty of a) consulting his local ordinary, and b) complying with his judgment when he states that the cleric's departure from the diocese will cause serious and unavoidable injury to souls. The major cleric is obliged to abide by these two restrictions of canon 542, 2° *pr.* Surely, in a wide sense at least, are they considered obligations placed upon him by positive ecclesiastical law for the fact that he is a major cleric.

I. Arguments in Favor of Canon 542, 2° *pr.* Binding Reduced Clerics

From the previous explanation of the nature and effects of reduction to the lay state, it is evident that the reduction applied by the Church is not intrinsic or theological, but extrinsic or juridical. Hence internally and in the sight of God these clerics remain firmly established in orders. It would not be rash at all to say that such externally reduced clerics are sufficiently constituted in orders to fall under the impediment, especially since the Code does not make any distinction in the impediment. Such an opinion could be confirmed by canon 211, §1, which states that sacred ordination once validly received is never rendered invalid. Moreover such an opinion is confirmed by the manner of re-admitting a reduced cleric to the clerical state. His re-admittance is by no means a repetition of the substantial rite of ordination, but is of the nature of a mere accidental ceremony.[71]

Legislation which indicates an existing bond between the reduced cleric and his proper bishop through incardination is found in canon 212. It states that, if a cleric in minor orders has returned for any reason to the state of the laity, he may again be admitted among the clergy with the permission of the ordinary into whose diocese he was incardinated by ordination. This same ordinary may grant permission only after a diligent inquiry into the life and character of the individual, and after a period of probation to be specified by himself.[72]

II. Interpretation of Canon 542, 2° *pr.*

In the face of the arguments presented, there is need to look elsewhere for a possible solution of the problem. In canon 19 are found rules of interpretation with respect to odious laws. They are to be interpreted in a strict sense. They are not to be extended to other cases, but are to be interpreted literally according to the proper meaning of the words. The canon states that laws which decree a penalty, or restrict the free exercise of a person's rights, or establish an exception from the law, must be interpreted in a strict sense.

History attests to the solicitude of the Church to safeguard the liberty of clerics to embrace the religious life. It

[71] Cf. can. 212; Wernz-Vidal, *Ius Canonicum*, II, p. 457, n. 395.

[72] Can. 212, §1: Qui in minoribus ordinibus constitutus ad statum laicalem quavis de causa regressus est, ut inter clericos denuo admittatur, requiritur licentia Ordinarii dioecesis cui incardinatus fuit per ordinationem, non concedenda, nisi post diligens examen super vita et moribus, et congruum, iudicio ipsius Ordinarii, experimentum.

§2. Clericus vero maior qui ad statum laicalem rediit, ut inter clericos denuo admittatur, indiget Sanctae Sedis licentia.

bears witness that the Church considers this liberty, as it were, a right belonging to every cleric.[73] It insists on his liberty to enter the novitiate and in the present legislation of canon 542, 2° *pr.*, lays down only two restrictions by which the major cleric must abide in order to be admitted licitly. For the case at hand, let it be considered as a right of a reduced cleric. With an application of canon 19, it would seem at first that canon 542, 2° *pr.*, could be called a restriction on that right, and that, as far as the cleric is concerned, the latter canon is an odious one. Hence it is subject to a strict interpretation, and thus does not include him, a person reduced from the clerical state. However, with canon 542, 2° *pr.*, regarded from the bishop's point of view, the legislation cannot be called odious; rather, it is to be deemed favorable, for it empowers him with a wider control over his clerics, even the reduced clerics, since they may still be considered as established in sacred orders (*constituti in sacris*). Consequently, according to canon 19, the reduced cleric on his part cannot be said to be held; from the bishop's point of view the cleric can be said to be held, since the bishop can use the wide interpretation of canon 542, 2° *pr.*[74] Since one inseparable law is constituted in the canon here in question, a further solution of the problem must be sought in canon 18, which furnishes the rules for the interpretation of doubtful laws.[75]

[73] Whether it is an inherent right of every Christian, and therefore of clerics, to enter religion when he is not suffering from an impediment is disputed. It is not the writer's intention to solve that question here. But if the reduced cleric can not save his soul outside the religious life, it would appear that he could claim it his right to be admitted and the community would have a grave obligation in charity, to say the least, to admit him.

[74] "Odia restringi et favores convenit ampliari."—Reg. 15, R. J., in VI°.

[75] Can. 18: Leges ecclesiasticae intelligendae sunt secundum propriam verborum significationem in textu et contextu consideratam; quae si dubia et obscura manserit, ad locos Codicis parallelos, si qui sint, ad legis finem ac circumstantias et ad mentem legislatoris est recurrendum.

Taking the text and context of the law of canon 542, 2° *pr.*, according to their ordinary and proper significance, one cannot but admit that even reduced clerics are among those constituted in sacred orders. Yet, for the obvious reasons mentioned, one must concede that a reasonable doubt and a certain degree of obscurity remain as to the effect of canon 542, 2° *pr.*, on them. As a result, the interpretation must be sought in parallel legislation of the Code.

A clear instance of parallel enactment of laws can be found in the relation between canons 542, 2° *pr.*, and 132. In a manner similar to the former, canon 132 opens with the phrase, "Clerics ordained to major orders" (*clerici in maioribus constituti*), and continues "are forbidden to marry, and are bound in such manner by the obligation of preserving chastity that sins against chastity are also a sacrilege . . ." Evidently, though, the legislator did not consider that law as binding a cleric reduced to the lay state, since in canon 213 he explicitly declares that the major cleric is still required to observe celibacy. As there is no such additional, singular enforcement of the impediment, canon 542, 2° *pr.*, should be regarded as not possessing any binding influence upon a major cleric reduced to the lay state. Apparently the legislator precisely indicated that the phrase *clerici in maioribus constituti* of canon 132 does not include the cleric reduced from major orders, for if he did consider him included, then the legislation of canon 213, §2, would be entirely and absolutely superfluous. Since nowhere in the Code can there be found a law similar to canon 213, §2, applying canon 542, 2° *pr.*, to reduced clerics, the impediment can be regarded as not exerting any canonical effect upon them.

Another parallel case can be found in the relation between canons 542, 2° *pr.*, and 135. The latter canon opens with the phrase, "Clerics, constituted in major orders, . . ." which is almost identical with the opening words of the former canon, namely, "Clerics constituted in sacred orders, . . ." Canon 135 proceeds to state that such clerics in major orders are bound by the obligation of daily reciting all the canonical hours, but that those clerics in major orders who have been reduced to the lay state, as described in canons 213 and 214, are not obliged to fulfill this obligation. What conclusion is to be drawn from this latter comparison of parallel cases? Is it to be said, as in the previous comparison, that the legislator does not intend to include among the clerics established in major orders those who have been reduced to the lay state? If so, reduced clerics would not be held to comply with canon 542, 2° *pr.* Or is it to be concluded that, unless the Code mentions them as excluded, or unless the legislator releases them from an obligation, they are still to be considered as falling under an obligation? If so, reduced major clerics are subject to the prescriptions of canon 542, 2° *pr.*, for therein is found no such exclusion or concession.

Whereupon recourse must be had to the purpose (*finem*) and circumstances of the law and the mind of the legislator. The end of the law is that motive for which the legislator makes the law. It is practically the common opinion of the authors who present any reasons at all that the provision demanding previous consultation with the local ordinary before entry into the novitiate is based on the canonical obedience required in canon 127.[76] However, a cleric in major orders reduced to the lay state is freed from this obligation of special respect and obedience.[77]

[76] Schaefer, *De Religiosis*, p. 440, n. 802; Berutti, III, p. 144; Gerardus Oesterle, *Praelectiones Iuris Canonici*, Vol. I (Romae: Collegio S. Anselmi, 1931), p. 291, who adds as additional reasons: "honestatem morum . . . et bonam educationem." Cf. Beste, ad can. 542, 2°; Wernz-Vidal, *Ius Canonicum*, III, 207, n. 254; A. De Meester, *Juris Canonici et Juris Canonico-civilis Compendium* (3 vols. in 4, nova ed., Brugis, 1921-1928), II, p. 432, n. 992; Blat, *Commentarium Textus Codicis* (3. ed., 1938), II, *De Personis*, pars II, p. 285, n. 298. Some of these authors add the word convenience or harmony (*convenientia*) to that of obedience, but for all practical purposes here that could be included under the word obedience.

[77] This the writer bases on the conclusions reached previously, namely, that the obligations of canons 124-144, except celibacy, cease with reduction to the lay state.

In other words, the end of the law is to preserve the promised respect and obedience to the local ordinary; but the writer concludes that this end exists no longer. What, then, must be the interpretation in this regard? It must be this that the end, the purpose served by the consultation, ceases adequately though negatively.[78] And whenever the purpose of the law ceases adequately though negatively only in a particular case, as for one or several subjects, the law does not cease. The reason is that laws directly concern the community, not individuals.[79]

Schaefer († 1948)[80] presented another reason which by the writer is considered appropriate and weighty, namely that the ordinary be enabled to provide for the filling of the office[81] upon the cleric's departure. Concerning the facts here contemplated, however, the office would be vacant by the fact of reduction,[82] the ordinary would be certainly aware of the reduction, and the reduced cleric would not be able to remedy the situation even if he remained out of the novitiate.

The second element of the impediment, the one and only cause for which the local ordinary may justly oppose entry to religion, is the grave spiritual harm which cannot in any other way at all be averted. This reason can never be

[78] "A law ceases *intrinsically* when its purpose ceases; the law ceases itself. Thus the law of abstinence from blood and things strangled, enacted by the Apostles in the Council of Jerusalem, to encourage the conversion of the Jews, since they held such foods in abomination, ceased *intrinsically* when this aversion ceased ... The end (either its purpose or its cause) of the law ceases *adequately* when all its purposes cease; inadequately, when only some particular purpose of the law ceases ... The purpose of the law ceases *contrariwise* when an injurious law becomes either unjust or impossible of observance; or *negatively*, when the law becomes useless; universally, when the purpose of the law ceases with respect to all subjects or the majority of subjects; or *particularly*, with respect to some individual."—Amleto Giovanni Cicognani, *Canon Law*, p. 627.

[79] Cicognani, *op. cit.*, p. 628; cf. can. 21.

[80] *De Religiosis*, 440, n. 802.

[81] Cf. canons 188, 1° and 584.

[82] Can. 213.

adduced as a result of the reduced major cleric's departure, since the office is already vacant, and the cleric is rendered juridically ineligible for it. The grave harm, if there be any, has already been caused and will not be remedied by his continued physical presence in the diocese.

But such arguments only force upon the mind a conclusion similar to the previous one. The purpose of the law ceases adequately though negatively only in this particular case of reduced clerics (as opposed to the universal cessation of the purpose of the law). Yet such cessation of the purpose of the law does not imply cessation of the law itself.

The historical circumstances surrounding this impediment would help little to interpret the application of canon 542, 2° *pr.*, for as an impediment it is entirely new in the Code. Neither were any references in history found concerning the connection between reduced clerics and a possible obligation to consult previously with their ordinary before entry into religion. To consider the mind of the legislator, which is another rule for interpretation of doubtful laws, would be quite difficult and a solution of the problem could hardly be expected therefrom in this case.

After this somewhat lengthy discussion on the extent of canon 542, 2° *pr.*, in respect to major clerics reduced to the lay state, it must be admitted that the problem remains unsolved and that the juridic status of reduced clerics as to this obligation is not clearly defined in the Code. Yet there are some clearly defined facts remaining and a solution will hopefully be sought among them. Canon 107 states that by divine ordinance clerics are distinct from lay people, though not all of the orders of the clergy are of divine institution. Canon 948 declares that in the Church through Christ's institution the reception of an order distinguishes the clergy from the laity for the purpose of providing for the government of the faithful and the ministry of divine worship. It is evident that the Church recognizes only two juridic states among its faithful, and they are distinct one from the other. Although a religious may belong to either state, no single person can belong to both of these states, or belong to one and only partly to the other, or partly to one and partly to the other. Just as the Church uses its power to establish a lay person, intrinsically and extrinsically, in the clerical state through the reception of tonsure,[83] so it similarly employs its power to reduce him extrinsically to the lay state.[84] Therefore in the eyes of the law he is considered a layman and free of the obligation on clerics in canon 542, 2° *pr*. The aforementioned wide interpretation of canon 542, 2° *pr.*, as made applicable for the bishop in view of the fact that this control would be favorable to him, does not obtain, for the bishop's interests do not enter the picture at all. It appears that they were lost when the major cleric was reduced to the lay state, since canon 542, 2° *pr.*, does not apply to lay persons.

Since in this article there are found thus far many reasons both for affirming and for denying the inclusion of reduced clerics under the impediment of canon 542, 2° *pr.*, it is indeed difficult to form a final judgment, since the reasons presented on both sides more or less mutually destroy each other's force. One is inclined towards one opinion with a well-founded fear that the other theory is true. Because of the intrinsic arguments for both contentions, the writer does not feel justified in choosing one opinion to the exclusion of the other. He does, however, offer a practical solution in holding that the problem at hand is in reality a doubt of law, according to canon 15. The doubt concerns the existence, the force and extent of the obligation of canon 542, 2° *pr.*, as regards major clerics reduced to the lay state.[85] The former canon decrees that all laws, including invalidating and inhabilitating laws, lose their binding force in a case of *dubium iuris*.[86]

[83] Can. 108.

[84] Cf. can. 211.

[85] Cf. can. 15: Leges, etiam irritantes et inhabilitantes, in dubio iuris non urgent; . . .

[86] Cicognani presents a clear example of the application of canon 15: "If there is question of a *dubium iuris* with regard to some im-

In looking through the Code one finds that ordinarily mention is made of reduced clerics whenever there is question of imposing or remitting obligations proper to the clerical state. Examples of this are noticed in canon 212, which treats of re-admittance to the clerical state; in canon 213, §2, on celibacy; in canon 214, on the release from the obligations of celibacy and the divine office; and in canon 135, also on the cessation of the breviary obligation.[87]

Canon 542, 2° *pr.*, however, evidently enough does not contain such a reference where one could reasonably expect it if reduced clerics were considered as included therein.

Whence, in the final analysis, the writer contends that canon 542, 2° *pr.*, in its application to major clerics reduced to the lay state is a doubtful law, and that consequently it applies only to priests, deacons and subdeacons who at the time of their admission into the novitiate have not been reduced to the state of the laity. Accordingly, the answer to the previously proposed question is that the subdeacon reduced to the lay state by a rescript is not obliged to comply with the restrictions of the impediment before he can licitly be admitted to the novitiate of the brotherhood.

In the question and answer above, the writer has purposely insisted on the possibility of admitting a reduced cleric to the novitiate of the brotherhood. It is only in the admission to such a novitiate that the question would arise. The reason for saying this is that hardly any religious community would allow entrance into the novitiate for the preparation of clerics a reduced cleric who has not been reinstated and who does not have the necessary permission from the local ordinary or the Holy See according to the

pediment [to marriage], by the express consent of the Church given in the present Canon [15], the principle applies: *a doubtful law is no law;* and by virtue of said consent, for the whole matter depends on the Church's consent, the marriage is valid. In other words, in a *dubium iuris* a doubtful law is not binding and the Church supplies in this regard."—*Op. cit.*, p. 587.

[87] Other legislation in regard to clerics reduced to the lay state is found in canons 123; 136, §3; 141, §2; 211; 648; 2305, §1; 2358; 2387.

norm of canon 212. And after a reduced cleric has once more been reinstated among the ranks of the clergy, he is surely bound by canon 542, 2° *pr.*, when seeking admission into the novitiate. The reduced cleric as a candidate for admission to the brotherhood novitiate need not previously nor subsequently be reinstated. While as a religious (*conversi*) he will have the obligations[88] and the privileges of a cleric,[89] he is still not considered a cleric in the true sense.[90]

III. Consideration of a number of Cases

The conclusion that canon 542, 2° *pr.*, does not extend to major clerics who afterwards have been reduced to the lay state gives rise to a number of related problems which flow from certain vindicative penalties, which the Church mercifully inflicts primarily for the repair of the social order violated by the delict, and secondarily for the correction and reformation of the individual delinquent.

1. The case of a cleric reduced to the lay state according to canon 214. Besides the manner of reduction to the lay state through a rescript, canon 211 mentions the decree or sentence of canon 214. This latter canon states that a cleric who has been forced through grave fear to receive a sacred order, and who afterwards, when the fear had been removed, has not at least tacitly ratified his ordination by exercising the same order with the accompanying intention of subjecting himself to the clerical obligation by this exercise of it, may be reduced to the lay state by a sentence of the judge with the effect that the obligations of celibacy and of the reciting of the divine office come to an end, provided of course that the coercion and the lack of ratification have been legimately proved. The coercion and the lack of ratification must be proved according to the norms outlined in canons 1993-1998.

The ordination itself, however, may be so affected by

[88] Cf. can. 592. [89] Cf. can. 614. [90] Cf. can. 108.

coercion or violence that the act performed is not a free act (*voluntarium*), i.e., that there is lacking free consent of the will to the act. Accordingly, the Code explicitly states that an act which a person performs as a result of an extrinsic force which he cannot resist is to be considered invalid.[91] If this is proved, then the ordination itself must be held to be invalid, and there can be no question of having effectively contracted any clerical obligations. Because of the absence of a valid ordination, it is evident that the person who receives a decree making a declaration to this effect does not fall within the scope of the impediment under consideration.

In the case, however, in which the obligations arising from ordination are impugned on the ground of grave fear which attended the ordination, this conclusion is not quite so evident. To prove the influence of grave fear, the Sacred Congregation of the Sacraments adopts either the judiciary or the disciplinary manner.[92] If the judiciary process is used, two conformable sentences are required.[93] If they are favorable to the cleric, he is automatically free from the clerical obligations and according reduced to the lay state. If the disciplinary process is employed, the Sacred Congregation will decide the question after an informative process has been conducted by the tribunal of the competent curia.[94] If the decision is in favor of the cleric, he is automatically free from the clerical obligations and reduced to the lay state.[95] Thus, as far as the impediment is concerned, such an ex-cleric is regarded to be in the same juridical condition as the one reduced to the lay state by a rescript. As a consequence, he is no longer bound by the restrictions of canon 542, 2° *pr.*, when seeking admission into the novitiate of a brotherhood in a religious community.

2. The case of a deacon dispensed for marriage by means

[91] Can. 103, §1.

[92] Can. 1993, §1.

[93] Can. 1998, §1.

[94] Can. 1993, §1.

[95] Cf. Sweeney, *The Reduction of Clerics to the Lay State*, pp. 151-153.

of the faculty made available in canons 1043-1044. With only a little knowledge of history and the weakness of human nature, it is not too difficult to envisage a case in which a deacon would rashly attempt a civil marriage and thereafter live in a sacrilegious union. After some years it may be supposed that he finds it almost impossible to separate from the woman, for a number of reasons, and that he continues his life of sin until his partner suddenly finds herself in probable danger of death. It may be surmised that he would summon to her bedside the pastor who would then dispense the deacon from the impediment of major orders and validate the marriage. Within a few hours, however, the wife may die with great grief of soul because of her wicked life. The deacon, shocked by the whole event and at the same time realizing his freedom, may now determine to enter a religious community to make amends for his own sins and those of others whom he has led into sin. Upon the latter's application for admission to the novitiate, the religious superior would demand, among other things, that the deacon consult first his bishop according to canon 542, 2° *pr.* But the deacon may express his opinion that he is no longer bound by this impediment. Which of the two is canonically correct?

Canon 1072 declares that major orders constitute a diriment impediment to marriage and that consequently a bishop, priest, deacon and subdeacon can never validly contract a marriage without a dispensation from the law of celibacy. In certain cases of emergency the Church allows local ordinaries or, if these cannot be reached, even certain priests to dispense deacons or subdeacons from the impediment of sacred orders. In danger of the death of one of the parties living in unlawful wedlock, whether it be the cleric or his partner in sin, for the peace of conscience of the parties local ordinaries may dispense a deacon or a subdeacon from the impediment of sacred orders after taking care to avoid all impending scandal, and if there be need also of a dispensation from the impediment of mixed religion or of disparsity of cult, to demand beforehand the required *cautiones.*[96]

In the same situations in which the local ordinary has the faculty to dispense, but only when the local ordinary cannot be reached, the pastor, the priest who assists at a marriage contracted according to a simpler form as allowed by canon 1098, 2°, and likewise the confessor have the faculty to grant a dispensation from the impediment of the orders of deaconship and subdeaconship. The confessor, however, must use his power in the act of sacramental confession and the effect of his granted dispensation will be of avail only for the internal forum.[97]

There arises then the question whether or not a dispensation granted according to the norms set forth contains also a reduction to the lay state. This problem has been the subject of some considerable discussion. According to Sweeney, however, it appears correct to say that such a dispensation contains an automatic reduction to the lay state.[98] In consequence of this opinion, the conclusion here adopted is that the cleric is free from the impediment of canon 542, 2° *pr.* He may begin his life of amendment and reparation in the religious brotherhood without previous consultation with his local ordinary.

A similar case with like consequences could be construed from canon 1045 in virtue of which local ordinaries, under the same conditions and with the same precautions, also enjoy the faculty to dispense if the impediment is discovered when all the preparations for the marriage have been arranged and the marriage cannot without probable danger of grave harm be postponed until a dispensation is obtained from the Holy See. This faculty is effective also for the convalidation of the marriage if the same danger is present

[96] Cf. can. 1043.

[97] Can. 1044.

[98] *Ibid.*, pp. 137-139; Philippus Maroto, *Institutiones Iuris Canonici*, Vol. I (3. ed., Romae: apud *Commentarium pro Religiosis*, 1921), 878-880.

in delay and time does not permit the making of recourse to the Holy See. Lastly, in the same circumstances, the pastor, the priest who assists at a marriage contracted in accordance with the norm of canon 1098, 2°, and also the confessor have the same faculty, but only in occult cases in which not even the local ordinary can be reached, or in which if he can be reached there is danger of the violation of the seal of sacramental secrecy.

3. The case of a cleric deposed according to canon 2303. Deposition, while leaving intact the clerical privileges and obligations derived from ordination, brings with it a suspension from office, and a disqualification for any offices, dignities, benefices, pensions and positions, as well as a privation of these, should the delinquent already possess them, indeed even a privation of such of these as constituted his title of ordination.[99] As natural death deprives a person of all advantages in the natural or physical order, so deposition deprives a cleric of all that he values in the social order of the Church. In one blow it obliterates all the titles a clergyman may possess, while the clerical state itself and its essential privileges and obligations remain for the deposed cleric.[100] The obligations, which are defined particularly in canons 124-144, were undertaken by the cleric in ordination and remain intact, as does the power of orders from which they emanate. Conversely, the cleric is freed of the duties and obligations connected with his former office, dignity, pension or position in the Church, since they depend for their existence upon his canonical commission. With its revocation in the fact of deposition, they too fol-

[99] Can. 2303, §1: Depositio, firmis obligationibus e suscepto ordine exortis et privilegiis clericalibus, secumfert tum suspensionem ab officio, et inhabilitatem ad quaelibet officia, dignitates, beneficia, pensiones, munera in Ecclesia, tum etiam privationem illorum quae reus habeat, licet eorum titulo fuerit ordinatus. §3: Poena depositionis infligi nequit, nisi in casibus iure expressis." The cases referred to are expressed in canons 2314, §1, 2°; 2320; 2322, 1°; 2328; 2350, §1; 2354, §2; 2359, §2; 2379; 2394, 2°; 2401.

[100] Findlay, p. 142.

low the same course.[101] Nevertheless, it must be remembered that deposition does not expel the delinquent from the clerical state.

If the true nature and severity of the punishment of deposition are understood by a deposed cleric, it can readily happen that through the inspiration of divine grace he will perceive more clearly the gravity of his serious mistakes of the past. Thereupon, wishing to repair the evil of former years and to safeguard himself as securely as possible against future lapses, he may seek admission to the novitiate of a religious institute. To the question whether a deposed cleric must comply with the prescription of canon 542, 2° *pr.*, the answer must be in the affirmative. He is established, intrinsically and extrinsically, in sacred orders, and accordingly comes within the scope of that impediment.[102] However, as long as the cleric remains without a dispensation from the vindicative penalty of deposition, it is hardly possible to see the reason for which grave harm to souls might be advanced. This statement is based on the fact that the deposed cleric remains suspended from the office and deprived of all his benefices, offices and dignities, while at the same time he is also rendered incapable of acquiring thereafter any ecclesiastical office or benefice whatever. The complete disqualification of such a cleric for any office, commission or duty constituted or exercised for a spiritual purpose within the Church is emphasized by the Code through its use of the term *munera.*[103] In brief,

[101] "Accessorium naturam sequi congruit principalis."—Reg. 42, R. J., in VI°; Findlay, pp. 156-157.

[102] It is to be noted that the impediment of canon 542, 2° *pr.*, alone is treated here. Hence no mention will be made of other suggested norms of action previous to admittance to the novitiate of the brotherhood, as the dispensations from the vindicative penalties of deposition, aggravated deposition, degradation (canons 2298, 10°, 11° and 2236) and irregularities, and the absolutions from censures etc. There is no question here, or in the following case (4), of reinstatement into the clerical state, for a deposed cleric, as also a cleric perpetually deprived of the right to wear the ecclesiastical garb, is never expelled from that same state.

[103] Cf. can. 145, §1; Findlay, p. 133.

the deposed major cleric, since he is not reduced to the lay state, is certainly obliged to conform to the restrictions set in canon 542, 2° *pr.*

4. The case of a cleric perpetually deprived of the right to wear the ecclesiastical garb, according to canon 2304. If a deposed cleric does not show signs of amendment, and especially if he persists in giving scandal and does not heed warnings, the ordinary may deprive him forever of the right to wear the ecclesiastical garb. This deprivation entails the privation of the clerical privileges and the cessation of the charitable support referred to in canon 2304, §2.[104] The Code introduces here an aggravated form of deposition to which canonists sometimes refer as the perpetual privation of the ecclesiastical garb. This designation, however, is not quite appropriate, for canon 2304 clearly indicates that this privation cannot legally exist apart from a previous deposition to which it brings added privations.

Perpetual deprivation of the right to wear the ecclesiastical garb does not itself reduce the cleric to the lay state. The deposed cleric remains constituted in the clerical state,[105] in consequence of which he must abide by the legislation of canon 542, 2° *pr.*, in its application to clerics in sacred orders. But since he is burdened with a juridic inability to fulfill any office or position in the Church,[106] it is, as in the previous instance, hardly possible to conceive a situation in which the deposed cleric's departure would bring grave harm to souls in the diocese. Should injury result from the fact of the vacant office, it is to be remem-

[104] Can. 2304, §1: Si clericus depositus non det emendationis signa et praesertim si scandalum dare pergat monitusque non resipiscat, Ordinarius potest eum perpetuo privare iure deferendi habitum ecclesiasticum. §2: Haec privatio secumfert privationem privilegiorum clericalium et cessationem praescripti can. 2303, §2.

[105] Ioannes Chelodi, *Ius Poenale et Ordo Procedendi in Iudiciis Criminalibus iuxta Codicem Iuris Canonici* (4. ed., rcognita et aucta a Vigilio Dalphiaz, Tridenti: Ardesi, 1935), p. 69, n. 52.

[106] Can. 2303, §1.

bered that the position is left unoccupied because the cleric is suspended, and not because he leaves the diocese. Nevertheless, in order to be licitly admitted into the novitiate of a religious community the deposed major cleric referred to in this case must consult his local ordinary.

5. The case of a cleric under the penalty of degradation. An ancient form of the reduction of clerics to the lay state is the one brought about by way of the penalty of degradation, which punishment is mentioned in the Code.[107] Canon 2305, §1, expressly states that degradation includes deposition, the perpetual deprivation of the ecclesiastical garb, and the reduction of the cleric to the lay state. Degradation can be inflicted only on account of a delict specified in law[108] or if the cleric, already deposed and deprived of the right to wear the ecclesiastical garb, continues to give scandal for a year.[109]

Degradation is called verbal, when by means of the condemnatory sentence itself all the juridical effects are present immediately upon the passing of the sentence, without the need of its further execution. Degradation, as contrasted to verbal, is real, when the solemnities in the Roman Pontifical are observed.[110]

In degradation, the reduction of the cleric to the lay state is a constituent element of the inflicted penalty of degradation. It connotes the specific difference between the penalty of degradation and the penalty of the perpetual deprivation of the right to wear the ecclesiastical garb.[111] The essential effects of the penalty of degradation are found directly and immediately in the penal reduction of the cleric to the lay state, his lifelong loss of the dignity of the

[107] Can. 211, §1: Etsi sacra ordinatio, semel valide recepta, nunquam irrita fiat, clericus tamen maior ad statum laicalem redigitur... poena degradationis.

[108] It can be inflicted for the delicts mentioned in canons 2314, §1, 3°; 2343, §1, 3°; 2354, §2; 2368, §1; 2388, §1.

[109] Can. 2305, §2.

[110] Can. 2305.

[111] Cf. canons 2304 and 2305.

sacred ministry, his perpetual rejection from the service of the altar, his everlasting restriction to a communion with the Church in the mere capacity of a layman.[112]

The Code itself indicates the enormity of this penalty in its determination of the delicts to be punished with degradation. Realizing the wickedness of his former life and the gravity of public scandal, a degraded major cleric may easily enough, with the assistance of abundant grace, be filled with deep shame and profound horror so that he may desire to embrace the religious life, wherein he hopes to serve God more generously and securely through the profession of vows. If the religious superior accepts his application, there need to be no worry about the demands of canon 542, 2° *pr.*, since a degraded major cleric is not held by its prohibition. The solution to this case is given for the same reason that any reduced cleric is not bound by the impediment of canon 542, 2° *pr.* And this reason is that the writer contends that the obligation, in respect to reduced major clerics, is a *dubium iuris.* But the obligation of such a doubtful law is said, in canon 15, not to have any binding force.

[112] Findlay, p. 221.

CHAPTER VII

CONSULTATION WITH THE LOCAL ORDINARY

Canon 542, 2° *pr.*: Illicite, sed valide admittuntur: clerici in sacris constituti, *inconsulto loci Ordinario* aut eodem contradicente ex eo quod eorum discessus in grave animarum detrimentum cedat, quod aliter vitari minime possit (italics added).

Consultation with the local ordinary by one of his clerical subjects in major orders is required for licit admission into the novitiate.

Article 1. Various Classifications of Local Ordinaries

Canon 198 furnishes the definition of the term, local ordinary, as used in ecclesiastical law. Unless explicit exceptions are indicated, the following, besides the Roman Pontiff, are meant: within their respective territories, a) the residential bishop, abbot *nullius*, prelate *nullius*, and their vicars-general; b) the apostolic administrator, vicar apostolic and prefect apostolic; c) the clerics who succeed to the vacant offices of the aforementioned ordinaries through the prescriptions of law, as the cathedral chapter, abbatial chapter, prelatial chapter, or the body of diocesan consultors before a vicar capitular himself; likewise the pro-vicar and pro-prefect in a vacant apostolic vicariate and apostolic prefecture; d) the clerics who succeed to the vacant offices of the aforementioned ordinaries (listed under a and b) through the legislation of approved constitutions, if therein it is determined upon whom devolves the government of a vacant abbacy *nullius* and prelacy *nullius*.[1]

These local ordinaries have jurisdiction primarily and directly in their specified place or territory, and consequent-

[1] Cf. Wernz-Vidal, *Ius Canonicum*, II, 426-427, n. 367. Major superiors of clerical, exempt religious institutes are designated by the single term, ordinary, because their jurisdiction is personal and extends directly over their subjects (Can. 198).

ly also over the persons of that same locality. Whence the major cleric who desires to be admitted into the novitiate must consult his proper, local ordinary.[2]

A. The Competency of the Vicar Capitular

If the episcopal see is vacant, it is sufficient for the cleric of the diocese to consult that local ordinary to whom falls the duty of the government of that diocese, vicariate, or prefecture.[3] To perceive the full impact of this principle, it is considered worthwhile to study its implications more thoroughly in regard to the vicar capitular or the diocesan administrator.

Is it correct to say that the vicar capitular is completely and canonically competent to be consulted about entry into religion by a major cleric? Possible reasons for raising the question are that in some cases, not entirely unrelated to the practice as set forth in canon 542, 2° *pr.*, the ordinary power of the vicar capitular is curtailed in as far as he is allowed to grant letters of incardination and excardination only with the consent of the capitular chapter, and then only after the episcopal see has been vacant for one year.[4] Almost the same prohibition is directed against the vicar capitular in respect to the issuing of dimissorial letters.[5] In fact, he is not even permitted to grant dismissorial letters to those to whom the bishop has refused the letters.[6]

Finally, if from the consultation the vicar capitular thinks himself not justified to oppose the cleric's intention, according to the norm of canon 542, 2° *pr.*, he is not able to ap-

[2] Minor clerics are not held by the restrictions of the impediment of canon 542, 2° *pr.*, although ordinary courtesy and equity as well as clerical reverence and obedience would require them to inform their bishop of their future plan.—Cf. Wernz-Vidal, *Ius Canonicum*, III, 207, n. 254; Eduardus Regatillo, *Institutiones Iuris Canonici*, Vol. I (3. ed., Santander, Sal Terrae: 1948), p. 387, n. 693; Schaefer, *De Religiosis*, p. 441, n. 803.

[3] Cf. Berutti, III, 144.

[4] Can. 113.

[5] Cf. can. 958, §1, 3°.

[6] Can. 958, §2.

point another pastor within a year to replace the present one who wants to transfer to the religious life.[7]

Is the vicar capitular, therefore, freed from all restrictions when he acts as the local ordinary in canon 542, 2° *pr.*, so that his power is equal to that of a bishop in the point under discussion? As a solution to the difficulties presented above, the following arguments deserve attention:

a) Where the lawgiver does not distinguish, there neither must the interpreter introduce a distinction. But canon 542, 2° *pr.*, simply makes mention of the local ordinary without distinctions of any kind. Unlike this unqualified canon just referred to are the laws of the Church entrusting to the bishop, to the express exclusion of the vicar capitular, the power of uniting parochial churches,[8] of conferring benefices[9] and of permitting an exchange of two benefices.[10] Since the law governing the impediment of canon 542, 2° *pr.*, makes no distinction, the vicar capitular may rightfully fulfill the prescriptions outlined therein for the local ordinary. In any event, canon 198 states precisely the same idea when it legislates that they who, according to the prescriptions of law succeed in the government of a diocese, are to be understood as local ordinaries unless an express exception is declared.

b) Although the vicar capitular cannot grant excardination to a cleric until a year after the vacancy of the episcopal see, and then only with the consent of the chapter,[11] the same restriction does not extend to the excardination given by law to a cleric through the perpetual profession of vows.[12] The writer contends that after the cleric has fulfilled the requirements of canon 542, 2° *pr.*, upon the profession of perpetual vows his excardination takes place automatically and is not conceded by the local ordinary.

[7] Cf. canons 1432, §2, and 455, §2, 3°.

[8] Can. 1423, §1.

[9] Can. 1432, §§1 and 2.

[10] Can. 1487, §1.

[11] Can. 113.

[12] Cf. canons 115 and 585.

In any event, admission to the novitiate is not the equivalent of excardination, since the latter is not effected until perpetual profession is made. Hence, among those designated by the term, local ordinary, in canon 542, 2° *pr.*, the vicar capitular is rightly to be included. He is not bound to wait a year or to obtain the consent of the chapter, before he can act according to the norm of canon 542, 2° *pr.*

c) Although the vicar capitular is somewhat restricted in regard to the granting of dimissorial letters, this same restriction cannot be extended to his action of giving counsel to, or opposing, a major cleric. The two cases can hardly be said to be parallel. Dimissorial letters connote the emerging of a new obligation for the diocese with reference to an additional cleric, while in the other case a departing cleric relieves the diocese of the earlier extant obligations in his regard.

d) While it is true that the vicar capitular cannot immediately appoint a pastor to the parish from which another one has left for the monastery, he can designate parochial vicars, and after the diocese has been vacant for the period of a year, he can also appoint a pastor to a parish of free conferal.[13]

In the light of these considerations, the writer holds that the vicar capitular has as full a right as a bishop in the matters of consultation and contradiction referred to in canon 542, 2° *pr.* If the vicar capitular realizes that the cleric can be spared without causing grave, spiritual harm to souls, he has no reason to oppose the cleric's departure for the religious life. Should he insist in his opposition for another reason, the cleric is nevertheless at liberty to enter the religious life licitly. Conversely, if the vicar capitular foresees grave, spiritual harm to souls as a result of the major cleric's departure, he is justified in his opposition, and can demand subjection to it if he cannot avert the injury by means of some other arrangements among the clergy.

[13] Cf. can. 455, §2, 1°, 3°.

B. The Competency of the Vicar General

Among those mentioned in canon 198 as belonging under the designation of local ordinaries is the vicar general. Since he is not expressly excluded from canon 542, 2° *pr.*, he must be regarded as canonically capable in respect to the consultation and opposition towards a major cleric intending to enter the religious life.[14]

Other arguments to prove this point could be advanced, but to a great extent they would be a repetition of those presented in proof of the competency of the vicar capitular. So it is thought unnecessary to proceed any further along the line of proving the vicar general's competency. And there is no plausible reason to doubt that he is fully empowered to act according to the specifications of canon 542, 2° *pr.*[15] However, it seems that a difficulty would surely arise when the vicar general judges that serious harm will be done to souls, inasmuch as the one who so judges is expected at the same time to try to avert any and all likely harm by means of other provisions or arrangements. Yet, in this his power is oftentimes restricted in that he has need of a special mandate.[16] For instance, he has need of the special mandate to fill a vacant ecclesiastical office,[17] to nominate and institute a pastor[18] and to permit the exchange of two benefices.[19] In view of this he would probably inform the bishop of the major cleric's intention. Then the bishop himself would want to make provisions for the prevention of the said serious harm to souls or would give the mandate to the vicar general if the latter needed it in making the arrangements.

Basically, however, in virtue of his office the vicar gen-

[14] Whether the vicar general holds his office under a governing bishop or whether he himself has charge of the diocese according to the provision of canon 429, §1, makes no practical difference.

[15] Cf. Berutti, III, 144.

[16] Can. 368, §1.

[17] Can. 152.

[18] Cf. canons 455, §3, and 1466, §2.

[19] Can. 1487, §1.

eral[20] is competent to clear the way for the cleric's licit entrance into the novitiate. His judgment as to the presence or absence of subsequent grave harm is sufficient, and the cleric may abide by it. Nevertheless, in exercising this authority, the vicar general is expected to pay heed to the warning of canon 369, which law cautions him not to use his powers in any way contrary to the mind and the will of the bishop.

Article 2. The Meaning of Consultation

For the purpose of arriving at a clearer notion of what the legislation means by the phrase, "without consulting the local ordinary (*inconsulto loci Ordinario*)," the positive aspect of the term consultation will first be studied. Thereafter it will be necessary only to observe the absence of this positive definition and the intent of the phrase will be revealed.

To begin with, the consultation of a major cleric with his local ordinary does not imply the asking of permission to leave the diocese in such a manner that upon refusal the cleric is bound to remain. This is evident from the very reference to the need of consultation rather than to the necessity of seeking permission. As canon 105 declares that it is sufficient for an ecclesiastical superior to consult certain persons when he acts in the name of a legal person, yet is not obliged to follow their suggested mode of action, so also canon 542, 2° *pr.*, manifests that it is sufficient for a major cleric simply to consult his local ordinary, and that he is not obliged to abide by the consulted one's suggestions.[21]

Is it correct to say that the required consultation is identical with the permission demanded, in some historical in-

[20] Cf. can. 368, §1.

[21] The writer, therefore, differs from the statement of Berutti, who says: "Quoties vero de clericis agatur qui saltem ad subdiaconatum iam promoti, . . . Ordinarii loci licentiam iidem habere debent antequam ad novitiatum admittantur."—*Op. cit.*, III, 144;; cf. Schaefer, *De Religiosis*, p. 440, n. 802.

stances, of religious who proposed to transfer from a less strict monastery to one more austere in its prescriptions of mortification and penances? Is the consultation, then, to be regarded as the equivalent of a permission which, while it must be sought, is not a prerequisite for action if it should be refused? History furnishes some instances of this type of permission, of which one is here presented.

Pope Julius II (1503-1513) in a constitution gave to the Minims of St. Francis de Paula (1416-1507) the privilege to receive into their Order religious of Mendicant or other privileged Orders, as long as these had first asked for permission from their superiors, either verbally or in writing, either personally or through some intermediary, and even though the permission had not been granted.[22]

Commentators were not wanting who demanded a like permission in view of the fact that a major cleric needed to consult the local ordinary before entering a religious institute. But as Nilles (1828-1907) observed,[23] they were led by the authority of the often cited canons, *Licet* and *Admonet* of the Decretals, which, however, did not specifically treat this particular point under discussion. The canon *Licet* applied to a religious who wished to transfer to an institute demanding observance of a stricter religious life. Although the canon *Admonet* forbade clerics in general to abandon their churches, Sanchez (1550-1610) with good reasons expressed belief that the restriction was not to be extended to clerics who intended to embrace the religious life. Otherwise the bishop would have been empowered to decide whether his priests were led by true zeal in seeking the transfer, and to deny his permission if he found it wanting.[24] Therefore the canon *Admonet* could not be ad-

[22] Const. *Dudum,* 28 iul. 1506—*Bullarum Diplomatum et Privilegiorum Sanctorum Romanorum Pontificum Taurinensis Editio* (24 tomes in 25 vols., Augustae Taurinorum-Neapoli, 1857-1872), V, 432.

[23] Nicolaus Nilles, *Selectae Disputationes Academicae Juris Ecclesiastici* (Oeniponte, 1886), p. 81 (hereafter cited as *Selec-Disputationes*).

[24] *Opus Morale,* lib. IV, cap. 25, n. 48.

vanced as an argument which proved that permission had to be asked by a major cleric who wanted to enter a religious institute.[25] Similarly, Pope Benedict XIV expressed the same intent in a decree of the Sacred Congregation of Religious, which dealt with the requirement of testimonial letters for all religious state. While bishops were asked to cooperate in providing the information concerning the qualities of their subjects, they were not allowed freedom to withhold the requisite testimonial letters.[27] There was no evidence that they were allowed a choice as to whether to grant or refuse the letters (as if the letters were to be given or denied like permission in regard to other important acts), much less was any indication given that the bishop's permission as such was needed for the candidate's licit entrance into the novitiate.

Another decree, in 1851, from the same Congregation emphasized the obligation of local ordinaries to provide the requested information: "Quid agendum sit, quando Ordinarii nolunt dare litteras testimoniales non aliam ob causam, nisi quia opponuntur ingressi Postulantis in religionem?" The answer: "Ordinarios,... non posse testimoniales litteras denegare; si tamen eas dare recusent, recurrendum erit ad S. Congregationem super statu Regularium."[28] This response once more indicates the duty on the part of the bishop to grant testimonial letters to lay and clerical aspirants to the religious life, and thereby implicitly proves that the concept of permission is not at all included in these letters.

[25] Cf. Fagnanus, *Commentarium in Tertium Librum Decretalium*, c. 18, X, *de regularibus et transeuntibus ad religionem*, III, 31, n. 28; Nilles, *Selectae Disputationes*, pp. 81 and 82.

[26] Ep. *Ex quo*, §13—*Fontes*, n. 374.

[27] S. C. super Statu Regularium, decr. *Romani Pontifices*, 25 ian. 1848, §§I, II—*Fontes*, n. 4375; Canon 544, §4, governing the reception of candidates who are clerics, omits the requirement of testimonial letters from those bishops in whose dioceses they have resided before ordination.

[28] S. C. super Statu Regularium, declar. 1 maii 1851, ad n. 6—*Fontes*, n. 4377.

As in the act of issuing of testimonial letters so also in that of the required consultation, there is hardly present any demand for permission needed by a major cleric to embrace the religious state.[29] Evidently, too, the required consultation specified in canon 542, 2° *pr.*, does not contain the need of permission such as was required of transferring religious, namely, that before a transfer the religious had to seek permission even though he would not be adversely affected by the fact that it was not given him.[30]

What, then, is meant in the present context by the term consultation? According to the words of Pope Benedict XIV, by consultation is to be understood the disclosure or manifestation of the major cleric's intention, together with the reasons in so far as their nature permits, so that the bishop may provide for the fulfillment of a future vacant position.[31] Adopting a similar interpretation, Larraona points out that the major cleric must inform his bishop of his intention and then listen to his counsel, objections and opportune observations. The same author calls attention to the fact that a mere notification sent the local ordinary to reveal the major cleric's proposal would not suffice to meet the requirement of consultation.[32]

This consultation is prescribed for priests and other major clerics holding important positions in the government of the diocese. Indeed, it is an obligation imposed in fulfillment of the natural law. For these clerics are minsters with the bishop in the Lord's vineyard and therefore they must cooperate so that their work will produce

[29] Much less is such "permission" required by a minor cleric or a seminarian without any Orders, for the reason simply that the impediment of canon 542, 2° *pr.*, pertains only to major clerics. *Supra*, pp. 55-56.

[30] Cf. Nilles, *Selectae Disputationes*, p. 81.

[31] Ep. *Ex quo*, §13: "... ante omnia debeat [presbyter] Episcopo consilium suum, eiusque capiendi rationes, quantum earum natura fert, aperire."—*Fontes*, n. 374.

[32] "Commentarium Codicis," *CpRM*, XVII (1936), 245; cf. Vermeersch-Creusen, *Epitome*, I, 503, n. 682; Wernz-Vidal, *Ius Canonicum*, III, 207.

the results demanded of their vocation.[33] Schaefer added another reason to the foregoing when he said that respect and clerical obedience towards the bishop require consultation before a major cleric can licitly be admitted into the novitiate.[34] Accordingly, even a major cleric who, for some reason or another, is not actively engaged in the work of the diocese is nevertheless bound to consult with his local ordinary before licit admission into the novitiate can be granted to him.[35]

Article 3. The Consultation of Canon 105 and Canon 542, 2° *pr.*

In regard to the consultation demanded in certain cases of an ecclesiastical superior before he acts in the name of a legal person, canon 105 clearly establishes what is meant when the law requires that a superior seek the counsel of specified clerics. If consultation alone is demanded, the canon states, it is sufficient for the validity of the action that the superior consults those who are indicated. He fulfills his obligation when he hears or asks the views of the respective parties concerning the action to be performed, so says Coronata, who goes on to state that, if the interrogated persons shall give no counsel, by that very fact they are considered as not having any opinion to offer. Consequently the superior can act validly and licitly without having received an explicit reply.[36] Furthermore, after having consulted the determined persons according to the method prescribed by law, the superior acts licitly even though in a manner different from, or opposed to, their suggestions.[37]

[33] Benedictus XIV, ep. *Ex quo*, §13—*Fontes*, n. 374.

[34] *De Religiosis*, p. 440, n. 802; cf. can. 127.

[35] Cf. Nilles, *Selectae Disputationes*, p. 85.

[36] Cf. Matthaeus Conte a Coronata, *Institutiones Iuris Canonici*, Vol. I (2. ed., Taurini: Marietti, 1939), p. 188, n. 153; Albertus Toso, *Ad Codicem Iuris Canonici Benedicti XV Pont. Max. Auctoritate Promulgatum Commentaria Minora* (5 vols., Romae: Jus Pontificium, 1920-1927), II, 54.

[37] Can. 105.

To some, perhaps, this demand for consultation might seem useless if the superior is not bound to follow even a unanimous decision. But this contention of the apparent futility of the consultation cannot be sustained. The purpose of the law is nevertheless obtained. For this is its main purpose: to prevent an ill-advised and injudicious act. And if a superior knows that he must make known his plans to a number of persons and will be obliged to hear their views on the matter, he will surely be careful and judicious in formulating his plans and methods for action. He will think twice before he presents a matter to the persons that need to be consulted, for he will want his proposals and methods of action to be in reality plausible and sound. With an open mind he will lay his problems before the specified persons and hear their views, for the judgment reached by two or more persons is of greater importance than that reached by one alone.[38]

Although the foregoing considerations relate to an ecclesiastical superior who by law must consult a certain person or group of persons previous to performing some act in the name of a legal person, yet by way of analogy the same prinicples can be applied to the consultation with his local ordinary required of a major cleric before licit admission into the novitiate can be extended to him. As there is only one person involved, it is considered sufficient in itself that the consultation be made personally or by letter,[39] or perhaps even by means of the telephone. Likewise, the cleric must consult his proper local ordinary, but if the latter does not make known his deliberations or even give a response of any kind within a reasonable time, the

[38] Cf. Coronata, *loc. cit.;* Charles Augustine, *A Commentary on the New Code of Canon Law,* Vol. II (44. ed., St. Louis: Herder, 1923), p. 35. If the counsel of only one person is required, Coronata says that the superior can make this consultation either by word or in writing. So, too, he can receive the interrogated party's personal answer by word or in writing.—*Ibid.,* n. 154.

[39] Cf. Larraona, "Commentarium Codicis," *CpRM,* XVII (1936), 245; Schaefer, *De Religiosis,* p. 440, n. 802.

cleric has fulfilled his obligation. With a clear conscience he can make application for admission into a religious institute. This the religious superior and chapter can licitly grant him. Should the local ordinary declare his refusal for reasons other than the one justifiable motive of grave harm to souls, the cleric possesses the same freedom of action. If, however, the local ordinary judges from the consultation that the harm contemplated in canon 542, 2° *pr.*, will result, he need only manifest his judgment and the major cleric will be expected to render him obedience. Although the cleric has discharged his duty of consultation, he is subsequently further bound by the bishop's judgment until the latter is enabled through some other arrangements to prevent the foreseen injury.

As said previously, the cleric who has taken the initiative in consulting his local ordinary will probably receive an immediate reply expressing the mind of the bishop in this matter. However, the local ordinary may want time to give more thought to the major cleric's proposition, a desire which is not unreasonable.[40] Yet prudence suggests an expression of the result of the bishop's deliberation on the matter within a reasonable time. The delay must not be a pretext for forestalling the cleric's departure. Can it be said that there is any limit to the period of time that the cleric must wait for a response?

ARTICLE 4. THE ELEMENT OF TIME AND CANON 1710

Whenever a person is obligated by law to seek the advice of another person, is it not correct to deduce that the latter has a corresponding obligation by that same law to declare his opinion when consulted? In canon 542, 2° *pr.*, an instance of such mutual obligations is contemplated. The same canon assumes that, according to the common practice of men, a response is given either immediately or soon after the matter has been submitted for decision. It does not,

[40] Larraona expresses this thought well: "Ac proinde locus, tempusque ac commoditas offerri Ordinario debent ut, quae in Domino censeat, manifestare valeat."—*Ibid.*, note 294.

however, give any indication of the length of time, when a period for deliberation is requested, that a major cleric must postpone action in expecting an answer to the manifestation to the local ordinary of his proposal to enter the religious life.

As the local ordinary realizes the intent of the legislator to guarantee the traditional liberty granted clerics to embrace the religious life, he, being of a similar mind, desires to safeguard the cleric's freedom. He wants to be careful not to voice his opposition to the pursuit of evangelical perfection in the religious life, except for the one and only canonical reason allowed, i.e., that grave, spiritual harm will be inflicted upon the faithful by the cleric's departure, which injury the local ordinary cannot avert by some other provisional arrangement in the diocese. Consequently, there can be no reasonable objection if the local ordinary wants time to consider the whole matter thoroughly. But for what length of time can he feel justified in deliberating over the major cleric's expressed intention?

It is not the writer's aim to set down a definite period as to days and months. Rather he would suggest a possible juridic norm gathered from an instance of ecclesiastical legislation in the fourth book of the Code, which indicates the insistence of the Church upon definite action when a party has the right to attention in law.

In regard to the admittance or rejection of a bill of complaint, canon 1709 directs the judge or court either to admit or reject as soon as possible the bill of complaint. When after one month from the presentation of the bill the judge has not issued a decree admitting or rejecting the same bill, the party may demand the issuance of such a decree. If, nevertheless, the judge is silent, the party may have recourse to higher authority upon the lapse of five days after submitting the petition in which he asked the judge to take action.[41] The one-month period within which the judge must admit or reject the bill of complaint is called a con-

[41] Can. 1710.

tinuous month to indicate that no interruption of this interval is contemplated.[42] In other words, the plaintiff has the right to have his case promptly considered and given the attention specified in law.

The major cleric, after having submitted his proposal to the local ordinary, also has a right to receive a reply from him within a reasonable length of time, if time for consideration was desired. Upon the lapse of that period of time he should not be bound any longer by the impediment, since he is entitled to judge that the local ordinary has nothing to say concerning the proposal, and to conclude that he has discharged his duty of consultation as required by canon 542, 2° *pr.* The suggestion of a maximum waiting period of one month has nowhere at any time been mentioned by any author. Therefore it carries no weight of authority, nor is it an entirely satisfactory argument based on analogy. But the writer presents it for what it is worth, as affording an objective norm.

Article 5. Other Considerations Relevant to Consultation

In accordance with the intended scope of this work, the juridical consultation of his local ordinary made by a cleric in major orders seeking admission into a religious institute has received a certain amount of attention in this chapter. Yet it is likely that there enters into the mind of the clerics the question as to how many other persons he ought to consult and for what period of time. A brief discussion, therefore, of this type of consultation which, it must be remembered, is not referred to in the Church's legislation, is regarded as being worthy of some consideration in this work.

Frequently a transfer from the ranks of the diocesan clergy to the religious life is considered, though quite wrongly, as a step most extraordinary, to say the least, if not imprudent and rash. But a candidate should be convinced

[42] Cf. can. 35.

that a religious vocation, which is the result of the operation of divine grace, does not and can not originate in a man's own works. This conception of a religious vocation applies similarly to those who are in the lay state and to those in the clerical state. Canon 107 corroborates the idea that aspirants to the religious life can come from among the ranks of the clergy as well as from the laity. Canon 544, §4, does not necessarily give the impression that a transfer is of rare occurance. Canon 542, 1° *ult.*, the result of abundant legislation in the past, as well as canon 542, 2° *pr.*, indicates that clerics' transfers in the past have been somewhat frequent and are not to be looked at askance. Because of the unfortunate circumstances in which a major cleric finds himself at times, he might think that he is a sort of misfit and that some time in the past he has made a wrong decision.[43] In a situation of this kind it can easily enough happen that a cleric should find himself opposed in his proposal to enter a religious institute, not on account of the one canonically justified reason mentioned in ecclesiastical law, but rather on account of some indefinite and arbitrary reason. In spite of this opposition, the cleric is at liberty to make application for admission to a religious institute. But the superior and the chapter of the latter, not wishing to introduce a practice which might possibly incur the displeasure of the local ordinary, might delay and even entirely refuse the acceptance of a cleric thus opposed by his ordinary. Consequently, the clerical applicant feels abandoned and at a loss as to what method of procedure he is to follow next. Possibly becoming doubtful of the correctness of his own judgment in favor of a religious vocation, he perhaps will undertake incessant

[43] The cleric may think that he should have embraced the religious life and therein prepared for the priesthood instead of doing so in a diocesan seminary for the secular priesthood. Yet it is not at all incredible that, in some instances, God should give first His grace of a vocation to the priesthood and only later the grace of a vocation to the religious life. Canon 107 leaves this matter open and indeterminate: clerics as well as lay persons can embrace the religious state.

consultations with many whom he expects to help him through the adverse circumstances of his unhappy situation. As to the advisability of taking counsel with many and deliberating for a long time before entering religion, St. Thomas Aquinas presented a clear and precise solution in answering the following objections:[44]

a) It does not seem praiseworthy to enter religion without consulting many persons and reflecting beforehand for a long time, for it is written: " 'Believe not every spirit, but try the spirits if they be of God.'[45] 'If it [this counsel] be of God, you cannot overthrow it, . . .' "[46] Therefore a searching inquiry before entering religion ought to be undertaken.

b) It is written in the Books of Proverbs: " 'Treat thy cause with thy friend, . . .' "[47] But a man's cause would surely seem to be one which involves a change in his state of life. So before entering religion, one ought at length to discuss the matter with his friends.

c) It is necessary that one consider very accurately his ability to renounce his passions, because Our Lord in making a comparison with a man who has a mind to build a tower says that the man first reckons the charges that are necessary, whether he has the resources to finish it, lest he become an object of mockery. Since it happens that some cannot completely renounce their passions, long deliberation and much consultation should proceed entry into the religious life.

St. Thomas Aquinas opened his refutation of the foregoing objections by stating that, upon our Lord's calling Peter and Andrew, they left their nets immediately and

[44] *Summa Theologica,* IIa-IIae, q. 189, a. 10.

[45] I John, IV, 1. This translation is taken from: *The Holy Bible Translated from the Latin Vulgate* (published with the *imprimatur* and approbation of His Eminence Patrick Cardinal Hayes, New York: C. Wilderman, Inc., 1938), (hereafter cited as Latin Vulgate).

[46] Acts, V, 39. Translation from the Latin Vulgate.

[47] XXV, 9. Translation, *op. cit.*

followed him.[48] "Such obedience as this," according to St. John Chrysostom, "does Christ require of us that we delay not even for a moment."[49] St. Thomas continued to prove the objections to be erroneous when he answered that "long deliberation and the advice of many are required in matters of doubt . . . , while advice is unnecessary in matters that are certain."[50] In regard to entrance into religion itself, he stated that: a) ordinarily it is a greater good than the life in the state of the laity, and that doubting about this is to disparage Christ's counsel; b) entrance into religion, when considered in regard to the strength of the person who intends to enter, leaves no room for doubt because of the divine assistance: "They that hope in the Lord shall renew their strength, thy shall take wings as eagles, they shall run and not be weary, they shall walk and not faint."[51] Yet if some special obstacles as bodily weakness, a burden of debts, or other like factors stand in one's way, there should precede the taking of counsel and deliberation with such as are likely to help and not hinder him; and c) in regard to which Order one ought to enter, as well as with reference to other matters also, one may take counsel with those who will not hinder one's way.

In a definite reply to the first mentioned exception, St. Thomas stated that they who are in religion may doubt whether a candidate is led by the spirit of God or moved by hypocrisy. Wherefore it is necessary for them to try the aspirant whether he be moved by the divine spirit. As for the candidate himself, he cannot doubt that the holy purpose is from the spirit of God.[52] Hence the intention of entering religion need not be tried whether it be of God.

To the second objection, St. Thomas replied that "even

[48] Matthew, IV, 20.

[49] Hom. XIV in Matth.—Migne, *Patrologiae Cursus Completus, Series Graeca* (161 vols. in 164, Parisiis, 1856-1866), LVII, 219.

[50] Translation by English Dominican Province.

[51] Translation by English Dominican Province.

[52] Cf. Ps. CXLII, verse 10.

as the 'flesh lusteth against the spirit,'[53] so too carnal friends often thwart our spiritual progress," as the prophet Micheas declares: "A man's enemies are they of his household.[54] The Angelic Doctor continued: " 'No man putting his hand to the plough, and looking back, is fit for the kingdom of God.' But he does look back who seeking a delay returns home to consult his kinsfolk."[54a]

St. Thomas disproved the third objection with an assurance that many examples exist which show that the misgivings of those who hesitated in the quest regarding the attainment of perfection were unreasonable.[55] Thereafter he quoted from St. Augustine: "On that side whither I had set my face, and whither I trembled to go, there appeared to me the chaste dignity of continency,...honestly alluring me to come and doubt not, and stretching forth to receive and embrace me, her hands full of multitudes of good examples. There were so many young men and maidens here, a multitude of youth and every age, grave widows and aged virgins... And she smiled at me with a persuasive mockery as though to say: 'Canst not thou what these youths and these maidens can? Or can they either in themselves, and not rather in the Lord their God?... Why standest thou in thyself, and so standest not? Cast thyself upon him; fear not, He will not withdraw Himself

[53] Gal., V, 17. Translation from the Latin Vulgate.

[54] VII, 6. Translation from the Latin Vulgate.

[54a] Luke, IX, 52. Translation, *op. cit.*

[55] "...adverte diligenter quod doctrina Auctoris excludens consilia circa sufficientiam virium non habentium speciale impedimentum, formalis est, et de ingressuro bene disposito intelligenda: et non aliter. Bona autem dispositio ingredientis est ista: ut omnem suam fiduciam sustinendi in religione ponat in Deo."—Cajetan's commentary on IIa-IIae, q. 189, a. 10—*Sancti Thomae Aquinatis, Opera Omnia, cum commentariis Thomae de Vio Caietani,* Tom. X (Romae, 1899). "Sed illi qui huiusmodi debita dispositione carent, quid facient? An debeant ad consilia recurre? Respondeo: Aut hanc dispositionem acquirant, orando, eleemosynis vacando, purificando conscientiam, lectionem Scripturae aut praedicationem frequentando. Aut non ingrediantur religionem utpote indispositi, nisi cum spe quod ingresso dabit Deus hanc bonam voluntatem, hanc sanctam fiduciam."—Cajetan, *loc. cit.*

that thou shouldst fall. Cast thyself fearlessly upon Him: He will receive and will heal thee.' "[56]

Evidently, therefore, St. Thomas was opposed to the advisability of taking counsel with many and deliberating for a long time previous to entry into religion. And should a major cleric feel himself abandoned through an unhappy situation such as the one described above, a suggestion that he should seek admittance to a religious institute in another part of the country might offer a possible solution.

A. Inducement of Others to Enter Religion

Since a certain amount of at least slight inconvenience is oftentimes inflicted upon the local ordinary when a major cleric departs from the diocese, it is important to regard briefly the former's attitude towards this troublesome condition. What is to be the mind of the local ordinary in clearing the way for his major cleric's licit entrance into religion? An expression of the position of St. Thomas Aquinas in this respect will be helpful. Although he did not refer directly to those who seek to remove the obstacles against a licit entry into religion, he did speak of those who, when given the opportunity, go even further by encouraging and inducing another to pursue evangelical perfection in the religious state. "Whether One Ought to Induce Others to Enter Religion" is the title of a separate article under the general topic which treats of the religious life.[57] In refuting the arguments which would impute as blameworthy such acts which draw others to religion, the Angelic Doctor answered: "It is written ([cf.] Exod. XXVI, 3 seqq.): 'Let one curtain draw the other.' Therefore one man should draw another to God's service... Those who induce others to enter religion not only do not sin, but merit a great reward. For it is written (James v. 20): 'He who causeth a sinner

[56] *Confessiones,* lib. VIII, cap. 11—*MPL,* XXXII, 760; *Summa Theologica,* IIa-IIae, q. 189, a. 10; translation by English Dominican Province.

[57] *Summa Theologica,* IIa-IIae, q. 189, a. 9.

to be converted from the error of his way, shall save his soul from death, and shall cover a multitude of sins'; and (Dan. xii. 3): 'They that instruct many to justice shall be as stars for all eternity.'"[58]

Such inducement, however, St. Thomas admitted, may be effected through a certain inordinateness, i.e., violence, simony and falsehoods,[59] which method might be the cause of a person's turning back on finding himself deceived. Thus the last state of that person could become worse than the first.[60] When the inducement to enter a religious institute is brought about through licit means, the Angelic Doctor observed, there is still available a time of probation wherein the candidate is tried in the hardships of the religious life. After employing other convincing refutations against the objections advanced, the same author concluded that it is not blameworthy, but rather praiseworthy, to draw others to the service of God in the religious life.[61]

[58] Translation by the English Dominican Province. Against those who uncanonically would prevent another from entering the religious life, Prümmer says the following: "Is, qui alium *vi, metu, fraude vel dolo* avertit ab ingressu in religionem, peccat contra iustitiam et ad restitutionem tenetur cum erga eum, quem avertit, tum erga religionem, in quam is voluit ingredi, si aliquod notabile damnum materiale inde ortum est. ([Cf.] S. Alphonsus Liguori, Theologia Moralis, lib. III, tract. V, n. 662). Is vero, qui alium avertit ab ingressu in religionem sine causa quidem rationabili, sed absque vi, metu, fraude, peccat graviter contra caritatem tantum. Ingressus enim in statum religiosum est magnum bonum et donum Dei. Sin autem quis a consequendo tanto bono indebite impeditur, magnum damnum patitur, immo aliquando in grave periculum salutis aeternae iniicitur."—*Manuale Iuris Canonici*, p. 269, q. 202; cf. Schaefer, *De Religiosis*, p. 431, n. 789.

[59] The third listed impediment in canon 542, 1°, legislates against the valid admission into the novitiate of persons who are compelled to enter a religious institute under constraint by grave fear, deceit, force, or who are admitted by a superior thus constrained. Canon 2352 inflicts a penalty upon those who coerce a person to embrace the religious state.

[60] Luke, XI, 26.

[61] Cajetan in his commentary on IIa-IIae, q. 189, a. 9, observed that the inducing of another to enter religion is an act good in itself, provided however that the person enters religion a) with a right motive, and b) in an institute where the religious life is exemplary.

B. Some Indications of a Religious Vocation in a Major Cleric

In the consultation between a major cleric and his bishop, the latter is not to be considered as a judge who is to decide the reality of a religious vocation in a cleric. He may, however, feel free to express his sincere convictions in this regard, which would not impose on the cleric any obligation of complying with them. In any event, if the local ordinary, besides taking the word of his cleric, could perceive some objective indication as to the presence of a religious vocation in his cleric, he might more readily do all in his power to clear the way for the cleric's acceptance of the religious garb. But are there any common and objective signs which would indicate a divine call of a cleric to the religious state?[61a]

It is evident that the signs of a religious vocation in a diocesan cleric are not the same as those that one can ex-

[61a] By reason of the title of this study, the writer must of necessity most frequently refer to the transfer of a cleric from the ranks of the diocesan clergy to that of the religious state. The almost incessant repetition of this transfer can lead to a wrong conclusion, i.e., that the religious state of perfection is considered much greater than the perfection demanded of the secular priests. It is true that Saint Thomas Aquinas and others hold that religious are in a state of acquiring perfection (*status perfectionis acquirendae*) and that bishops are in a state of exercising perfection (*status perfectionis exercendae*). But they do not contend that diocesan priests are in either one of these categories. In consequence however of the present developed ecclesiastical legislation, according to their own definition of perfection, the diocesan priests can be said to belong to a state of perfection similar to that of the bishops', i.e., *status perfectionis exercendae seu servitii.* The Rev. Claude H. Dukehart, SS., who wrote an excellent work in the School of Sacred Theology on the *State of Perfection and the Secular Priest,* embodied much canonical legislation with theological principles and concluded that this opinion is not so much against that of St. Thomas, but rather an extension of his thought, which he considers justified in the light of the present developed Church law. —Claude Dukehart, *State of Perfection and the Secular Priest,* The Catholic University of America Studies in Sacred Theology, 2. series, n. 46 (Washington, D. C.: The Catholic University of America Press, 1949, micro-carded 1950), pp. 213-214.

pect to find in a lay person, neither are they as easily recognizable. Clerics and religious do possess many practices and spiritual convictions in common, which are quite different from those proper to the laity, for instance, the flight from worldly pleasures and a great attraction to genuine piety. By this very training and education in the seminary, the diocesan cleric acquires a deep knowledge of the true worth of personal sanctity. This understanding of the real value of true holiness draws him towards interior perfection for the love of God. Thereupon a difficulty can easily arise as to whether this spiritual perfection is to be sought more intensely in the priesthood itself or in the religious state of perfection.[62]

The author, Peinador, writing in the *Commentarium pro Religiosis et Missionariis,*[63] treats rather thoroughly the topic of probable signs of a religious vocation in a cleric. For the main part, the rest of this article is a brief summary of his trend of thought in this regard.

No one who admits the truths of a divine vocation to the religious life can deny that there are certain indications in a cleric which give assurance of God's will calling him to the religious state of perfection, although the signs would not always provide moral, much less absolute, certitude. But whatever these indications are, they should declare a fitness of the cleric for the religious state and at the same time suppose an ineptitude for the diocesan priesthood.[64]

[62] Because of the very intimate and personal obligations frequently involved, a cleric might do well to mention his intentions together with his difficulties to his confessor or spiritual moderator who, acquainting himself with the motives and general qualities of the possible candidate to the religious life, would be well qualified to offer helpful advice concerning a religious vocation.

[63] "Sacerdotium Saeculare et Status Religiosus . . . ," XX (1939), 313-327.

[64] "Cum, enim, vocatio sit a Deo, et Deus sibi non contradicat; cumque vocatio ultimo dignoscatur ex *aptitudine integrali* ad aliquem statum, aptitudo ad unum dicit ineptitudinem, sive improportionem ad alium."—Peinador, *ibid.*, note 153.

Signs of a possible religious vocation in a cleric can be sought among the following: a) habitual weariness in secular work necessarily connected with the priesthood; b) a constant will to lead a more fervent life; c) singular difficulty with temptations in the world; and d) a lack of skill in the performance of pastoral functions. A fuller treatment of these indications will now be presented.

a) A habitual weariness in performing the secular work in diocesan positions, if accompanied with an interior fervor and diligent solicitude in priestly ministrations,[65] can be looked upon as a probable sign of a religious vocation in a diocesan cleric. At the least, such continual weariness would offer a justifiable reason for doubting the complete absence of a divine calling. If this disposition, however, does not have connected with it an inclination towards entering the religious state, the almost certain conclusion is that religious vocation is not at all involved in this instance. Rather, such weariness can be said to be the result of a natural sensibility and temperament, which is destroyed neither by grace nor by the priesthood. Nevertheless, granted the existence of the aforementioned inclination to the religious life, the continual tediousness would be a sufficient reason to assume the presence of a probable religious vocation.

b) A constant will to lead a more fervent life, if enkindled by a study of the religious life and its spiritual advantages, can be an indication in a cleric that he is called to the same state. As a place in which to surmount inquietude and spiritual difficulties, the cleric might find the worldly environment little conducive to the fulfillment of his resolution to lead a holier life. If his ardent desire

[65] "... aptitudo quam supponit vocatio non habet necessario adnexam delectationem in explendis officiis proprii status. Qui, enim, v. gr., religiosi sunt ex vera vocatione holocaustum Deo offerunt, quod non sine dolore magno fit. Attamen, *ordinarie*, id est, seclusis statibus animi *purgationis passivae*, difficultates in exequenda vocatione excludunt taedium proprie dictum, quod potius dicit aversionem voluntatis, quam *violentiam ad vincenda onera* obligationum."—Peinador, *ibid.*, note 154.

arises, not from a consideration of the religious state, but from a realization of the excellence of holiness in a minister of God, that desire can be said to be the effect of grace which is calling the cleric to a more generous love and faithful service in the sacerdotal minister.

Such a continual and persevering desire to live a more fervent life, when enkindled by a consideration of the religious state, can be a probable and even certain indication of the vocation, except in singular cases wherein clearer arguments point to the absence of the same calling. It is said to be probable because of other possible reasons which might justify a doubt as to the requisite qualities of the candidate, or because of the person's will which lacks sufficient constancy and determination to lead a more ardent spiritual life. Frequently, however, the previously mentioned indication is strong enough to warrant moral certitude as to the reality of a divine call. In fact, experience shows that this persistent will to live a more fervent life is oftentimes the motivating reason for the transfer, or as least such a desire ordinarily accompanies the transfer, of a cleric to the religious state.

c) Singular difficulty in overcoming the temptations of the secular life can also be a justifying reason for entering the religious life.[66] It is assumed of course that the gravity of the temptations is not occasioned by the cleric's own negligence and laxity. Rather, it is supposed that the cleric struggles courageously and consistently, but with very little success. Undoubtedly, such a cleric would discover a great opportunity for spiritual security in the profession of vows and in the fraternal companionship of the members in a religious community.

d) Incompetence in regard to the performance of pastoral duties, if yet there persists a sincere desire for spiritual

[66] "... pericula quaedam pro spirituali perfectione inveniri de se in pastorali ministerio. Quamvis *obiective* haec gravia sint, patet graviora vel minus gravia relative esse posse, subiectivis attentis conditionibus sive naturalis temperamenti, sive voluntariae curae vel negligentiae in illi obeundis."—Peinador, *ibid.*, note 164.

perfection, can form an adequate cause to indicate the presence of a vocation to the religious life. By the phrase "pastoral duties" are here included all the various obligations which demand the attention of a parish priest.[67] The reason for saying that a religious vocation can be expected in a case of this kind is that the religious state, not necessarily each individual order or congregation, offers a wide choice for the application of special capabilities. Among the religious orders and congregations, there are monasteries whose members undertake in varying degrees different kinds of work in their apostolate of serving God and bringing souls to Him. A cleric may as a religious enter a contemplative or an active life, or one in which there is a discreet combination of activity and contemplation. He may thus embrace that type of religious life which appeals most to him. The ineptitude for the performance of parochial duties surely cannot always be said to apply to the execution of the obligations of a religious institute, least of all if the cleric is not rash or ill-advised in his choice of a religious order or congregation.

Prior to the concluding of this article, it is regarded as worthy of repetition to observe that none of the previously described four signs or indications of a religious vocation in a diocesan cleric can be said to be such in an absolute sense. Yet these signs are helpful indications in the search regarding whether or not a cleric has been favored with the blessing of a vocation to the religious life.[68] Moreover, a transfer from the secular clergy to the religious state by no means can imply the loss of a priestly vocation. While

[67] "Saeculares, quia in saeculo degunt, implicari debent in pluribus negotiis vel officiis, ad quae non omnes apti convenienter sunt. Uti, ex causa, rationes sociales, vita publica, consortium familare, oeconomia domestica, displicent positive aliquibus. Ista, tamen, in vita saeculari sunt."—Peinador, *ibid.*, note 166.

[68] In the article, "Sacerdotium Saeculare et Status Religiosus . . .", *CpRM*, XX (1939), 313-327, Peinador offers some practical suggestions for retreat masters and confessors who are called upon to assist a cleric who for one reason or another finds it difficult to decide whether or not he is called to the religious life.

retaining the basic privileges and obligations conferred on him by ordinations, the cleric relinquishes his own diocese and attaches himself to a religious community. He preserves, juridically and theologically, the character of the priesthood imprinted on his soul, while he embraces a life in which spiritual perfection is to be sought by those who adopt that mode of life.

CHAPTER VIII

THE LOCAL ORDINARY'S OPPOSITION TO A CLERIC'S ENTRANCE INTO THE NOVITIATE

Canon 542, 2°: Illicite, sed valide admittuntur: Clerici in sacris constituti, inconsulto loci Ordinario aut *eodem contradicente ex eo quod discessus in grave animarum detrimentum cedat,* quod vitari minime possit; (italics added).

This canon determines the one and only reason for which the local ordinary is justified in opposing the entry into the novitiate by one of his clerics in major orders. The single cause is that on account of a cleric's departure from the diocese an injury, and that indeed a serious one, will result to souls, which harm cannot in any other manner be avoided. Evidently, too, this canonically justified motive for opposition endures only for the time during which the grave, spiritual harm would result. The bishop must try to find other ways or provisions to prevent such harm, so that his cleric may embrace the religious life.

Among the many authors consulted, it is found that besides restating in different terminology the idea of this particular phrase of the impediment they add very little of necessary explanation. For this reason, it is considered advisable to obtain a precise definition of the important words employed. After this clarification, the use of the word, *detrimentum,* in the Code will briefly be considered. Then the common spiritual good will be considered in its relation to the impediment. Following this threefold procedure, the writer hopes to present a clearer explanation of the second part of the impediment.

ARTICLE 1. DEFINITION OF THE WORDS *Cedat* AND *Detrimentum*

The verb *cedat,* from *cedo,* has a rather extensive meaning. From the many and varied definitions given, the following are considered to express the meaning as employed in this canon: to eventuate, to yield, to allow, to result, to occasion, to cause.[1]

The word *detrimentum* is defined as loss, damage, detriment. The departure of a cleric from the service of the diocese, therefore, must be the occasion of a grave detriment resulting for souls. The spiritual damage must be of such a nature that it can reasonably and prudently be perceived. The accompanying damage is much different from the possible material loss feared from a building or tree which threatens to collapse or cause serious damage. The mere threat in the latter cases gives a person the right to institute the action *de damno infecto.*[2] In the former case, much more than a mere theratening or menace is involved. The subjunctive mood, *cedat,* in this instance is used express the thought or opinion of another.[3] In consequence the writer holds that the grave harm to souls must readily be perceived by the local ordinary as being at hand, to happen presently as is indicated by the present, and not the future, tense of the verb *cedat.* The grave harm

[1] Cf. Rudolf, Köstler, *Wörterbuch zum Codex Iuris Canonici* (München: Verlag Josef Kösel & Friedrich Pustet, 1927-1929) s. v. *cedere*: von statten gehen, ausschlagen . . . ; E. A. Andrews, *Latin-English Lexicon* (Harper Brothers: New York, 1870), s. v. *cedo.*

[2] Cf. canon 1678. Another word very similar to *detrimentum* in its meaning and definition and frequently used in the Code is *damnum,* e.g., publicum animarum damnum, can. 2229, §3, 3°; compensatio d., canons 1731, 1°, 1653, §4, 1017, §3; querela d., can. 1939, §1; actio d. infecto, canons 1676, 1678; quaestio d. timere, can. 1674; d. vitare, can. 1530, §2; d. avertere, can. 1678; d. afferre, canons 1470, §1, 1°, 1625, §1; d. pati, can. 1832; d. reparare (sarcire, resarcire, compensare), canons 2355, 1704, 1°, 2211, 1476, §2; d. sequuntur, can. 2144, §2; d. imminet, can. 1678; d. oritur, canons 2213, §3, 1159, §1; d. ecclesiae obvenit, can. 1528; in d. vergere, can. 1479; teneri d., can. 1798, 1681—Köstler, *ibid.*, s. v. *damnum.*

[3] Cf. F. Schultz, *Latin Grammar* (36. ed., New York: : Frederick Pustet Co., Inc., no date), p. 235, §261: "Relative clauses take the *subjunctive* when they express the *thought* or *opinion* of *another* (not the opinion of the author). The use of *quod,* because, with the subjunctive is common with such clauses."

must follow as a necessary sequence from the conditions created by the cleric's departure.

Furthermore, the resultant harm to souls must be grave. Any inconvenient, disagreeable or even troublesome situation which might occasion only slight harm to souls, if any injury at all, does not suffice as a reason to oppose a cleric's entry into religion. Neither would a negative quality, such as the privation of a greater good, prove sufficient. For instance, the fact that several devout penitents could no longer make their devotional confession of sins twice a week could indeed be considered the privation of a greater good. Yet the impossibility of such frequent devotional confessions when occasioned by a cleric's entrance into religion would hardly result in grave spiritual harm to these penitents. Accordingly such a circumstance would prove insufficient for holding off a cleric from entering the religious state of perfection. On the contrary, a positive and grave detriment to the welfare of souls is postulated.[4] The inflicting of such damage can be found in the encouragement and advancement of evil or the privation of the supernatural means of salvation. The advancement of evil might result from a lack of sermons and catechetical instructions. As Christ has instituted certain supernatural means for salvation, e.g., the Church and its seven Sacraments,[5] a prolonged privation of such means in favor of God's creatures would readily inflict serious damage upon their spiritual life.

ARTICLE 2. THE USE OF THE WORD *Detrimentum* IN THE CODE

In the legislation of the Code there are found several instances in which the term *detrimentum* is employed. In a church committed to the charge of a rector, he is not permitted to hold parochial functions.[6] He may, however,

[4] Cf. Larraona, "Commentarium Codicis," *CpRM*, XVII (1936), 245.

[5] H. Noldin and A. Schmitt, *Summa Theologiae Moralis* (27. ed., 3 vols., New York: Frederick Pustet, 1940-1941), I, p. 22, n. 18 (hereafter cited as Noldin-Schmitt).

[6] Can. 481.

celebrate even solemnly the divine services, observing the laws of the founding of the church, although these services may not be so conducted as to injure the parochial ministry of the parish within whose boundaries the church is located. The bishop has the right to judge, in case of doubt, as to whether injury of this kind is done, and to prescribe opportune norms to remedy the harmful situation.[7]

The Code, therefore, connects injury (*detrimentum*) with interference directed against a pastor's rights which are noted in canon 462.[8] This canon refers to the administration of baptism, the Holy Eucharist, Holy Viaticum, extreme unction, matrimony; it concerns the pastor's right to assist at funerals, to bless houses and the baptismal font on Holy Saturday, and to conduct public processions. Should the rector illegimately interpose himself between the pastor and his performance of these reserved functions, the Code would designate the result of this uncanonical behavior with the word *detrimentum*.

Canon 1345 prescribes one of the opportune norms referred to in canon 482 to remedy a delicate situation.[9] If part of the faithful attend Holy Mass offered in the public oratory of exempt religious, the local ordinary may command, even through diocesan statutes, that these same religious impart an explanation of the Gospel or of some other Catholic doctrine. Accordingly, the implication is that the lack of catechetical instructions (which might well include sermons, too) in these churches causes a spiritual detriment, a problem which the local ordinary has a right to solve for the good of the faithful. The interference in parochial functions can be the occasion of detriment to ecclesiastical discipline. The neglect of catechetical instructions and sermons results in an injury to the apostolate of teaching divine truths.

Moreover, the Church wisely legislates to protect the

[7] Can. 482.

[8] Cf. Wernz-Vidal, *Ius Canonicum*, II, p. 955, n. 748.

[9] Cf. Wernz-Vidal, *Ius Canonicum*, II, p. 956, n. 749.

faithful from similar spiritual harm by obliging the pastor to live in the parochial residence near his church. Only the ordinary may permit him, for a just cause, to live elsewhere, provided even then that the house is not so far away from the parochial church that the performance of his pastoral duties is inconvenienced and suffers damage.[10] Although the pastor is allowed a two-month's vacation every year, he is bound to leave the parish in the care of a vicar substitute. Even if the pastor will be absent for less than a week he must provide through some arrangement for the needs of the faithful.[11] Illegitimate absence from his parish by the pastor deprives him of the fruits thereof for the time of his illicit non-attendance on his ministry. In fact, he may be deprived of the benefice itself according to the norms of canonical procedure,[12] during which the bishop at the expense of the pastor should provide for the faithful in order to forestall *detrimentum* to the salvation of souls.[13]

Whenever the pastor gravely neglects the administration of the sacraments, the care of the sick, the instruction of the children and the people, the duty of preaching on Sundays and holy days, or the custody of the parochial church, of the Blessed Sacrament and of the holy oils,[14] the ordinary shall proceed against him in the canonical manner prescribed in the Church's legislation.[15] In directing that this penalty be inflicted upon a negligent pastor, the legislator, it is true, does not give the reason that injury was caused directly to souls. He does indicate, though, that the negligence in the care of souls is the reason for the penalty. And if negligence in the care of souls is to be punished,

[10] Can. 465. §1: Parochus obligatione tenetur residendi in domo paroeciali prope suam ecclesiam; . . . non ita distet ut paroecialium perfunctio munerum aliquid inde detrimenti capiat.

[11] Can. 564, §§2, 4, 5, 6.

[12] Can. 2381, 1°, 2°.

[13] Can. 2168, §1.

[14] Cf. canons 467, §1; 468; 1329-1333; 1334; 1178; 1265-1273; 735.

[15] Cf. can. 2382.

the only reason for this penalty is that these same people will suffer consequent spiritual injury from the lack of attention.

The fact that detriment is to be viewed as resulting from illicit inroads made upon the reserved parochial functions makes one realize the close connection of detriment with a disordered performance of parochial functions. A pastor's serious obligation of residence and the penalties inflicted for its violation, and the serious punishment imposed for negligence in the performing of pastoral functions clarifies the importance of the pastor's spiritual ministrations. In truth, the importance of any priest's labors in the vineyard of the Lord is thus emphasized. The aforementioned penalties portray the zeal of the Church to protect the orderly and efficient exercise of pastoral functions for the good of the faithful. Conversely, the Church rightly frowns upon and punishes negligence which impedes the efficient performance of the acts incumbent on the pastor. The fact that the Church proceeds so severely against negligent pastors furnishes a clear insight into the Church's mind concerning the importance of priestly ministrations and the salvation of souls when it limits the liberty of clerics to enter religion.

The single word, *detrimentum,* is also employed in canon 605, by which all who have the custody of the cloister shall carefully be on their guard that, during the visits of strangers, the discipline shall not be disturbed or the religious spirit suffer damage (*detrimentum*) through useless conversation. A similar damage is referred to in canon 1334, the legislation of which justifies the bishop to request the assistance of religious for the imparting of catechetical instruction to his people, if he judges their help necessary for this work. The religious are obliged to give the petitioned assistance, especially in their own churches. Yet the help need not be extended if it is the occasion of detriment to religious discipline.

Canon 1162, §3, rules that a new church may not be

erected if its establishment brings *detrimentum* to the churches already existing, unless there is a proportionate spiritual benefit to the faithful. Wherefore, the ordinary before giving his consent must hear the rectors of the neighboring churches that may be concerned. In regard to the administration of ecclesiastical funds, canon 1523, 1°, requires that the administrators fulfill their office with the diligence of a good father of a family. Hence they must guard against any loss or *detrimentum* to the ecclesiastical goods confided to their care. Inefficient administration of the ecclesiastical temporal goods is one of the reasons for the removal of a pastor of non-revocable tenure. If a great loss results from such maladministration and the ordinary cannot remedy the evil either by depriving the pastor of the administration or by putting him under restraint in some other manner, even though in other respects the pastor fittingly exercises the spiritual ministry, then there is a sufficient cause for his removal.[16]

Other reasons, in a few words, which are sufficient for the removal of a pastor are incompetency and permanent infirmity which incapacitate the pastor from properly discharging the duties of his office, hatred of him on the part of the people, loss of reputation, or a porbable occult crime. Should the pastor want to attack the reason for removal adduced in the invitation to resign, he may seek a delay to prepare proofs, which postponement the ordinary may grant at his discretion, provided that no hurt to souls (*detrimentum animarum*) is caused thereby.[17]

Primarily, these five examples have been presented in aid of the reader's more facile understanding of the manner in which the Code uses the word *detrimentum*; yet a worthwhile observation can be made regarding the implication indicated in canon 2147, 5°, as related to canon 2151, i.e., that the Code vouches for the possibility that an inefficient administration of temporal goods may directly be the oc-

[16] Can. 2147, 5°.
[17] Can. 2151.

casion of spiritual harm to souls, the decision concerning which is confided to the local ordinary in the latter canon. In consequence, it is contemplated by the legislator that a condition brought about by a cleric's permanent departure from his diocese may be of such a nature as to be either the immediate or the mediate occasion of grave harm. When a major cleric's entrance into religion is the immediate occasion of serious spiritual injury to the faithful, the bishop has the right to oppose his departure from the diocese. When a major cleric's entry into the novitiate is the mediate occasion of similar harm, the same power is given the bishop for the duration of such harm.[18] Hence, a major cleric not directly associated with the charge of souls can by his departure be placing a condition which indirectly, or mediately, yields to or causes serious harm to souls.

In concluding the previous two articles the writer holds the following concerning the detriment and its postulated gravity. The major cleric's departure must be the direct or indirect occasion or cause of the spiritual injury. Among circumstances that may lead to the said harm are the lack of any priestly ministrations designed for the welfare of the spiritual life of the faithful, e.g., the lack of such sacerdotal functions as catechizing, preaching, caring for the sick, administering the sacraments, taking care of the administration of church property. The lack of such priestly functions must of course extend over a certain period of time, depending on the importance of the work for the faithful, before the damage to souls can be said to be serious. In the previously cited five examples of the use of the word *detrimentum,* not once was it used with the qualifying adjective, grave. Only in canon 542, 2° *pr.,* is the word "detriment" modified by the adjective "grave."

[18] However, when the local ordinary clearly foresees this injury to souls resulting either immediately or mediately upon the cleric's departure, he may not let the case rest there. He must try by other arrangements to provide for the removal of this threatening damage, so that his clerical subject who has a religious vocation may be freed from restrictions to follow his calling. Cf. *infra,* pp. 157-159.

This fact justifies the opinion that the legislator was careful to impart the idea that a really grave injury was postulated if the liberty of a cleric to enter a religious institute was to be curtailed. Moreover, since the Code uses the plural form, *grave animarum detrimentum,* the injury must result for several people, at least more than one, to justify the local ordinary's opposition.

ARTICLE 3. THE COMMON SPIRITUAL GOOD OF THE FAITHFUL

If the motivating reason for the restriction of a major cleric's freedom to enter the religious life is sought, it can be discovered in the principle that ordinarily the public good is to prevail over the private good.[19] This preference of the public good to one's own private interests is clearly attested in an ecclesiastical document governing the oath required for the "title of the mission."[19a] In the formula of the oath the ordinand obliges himself not to enter any regular Order without special permission of the Holy See or of the Sacred Congregation for the Propagation of the Faith. The reason for this was to let the Holy See judge, after hearing the opinion of the ordinary of the particular locality, whether or not the mission to which the cleric was attached needed him so badly that he could not be spared, because the public good should take precedence over the private.[20] Accordingly, without the special permission of the Holy See or the Sacred Congregation for the Propagation of the Faith he could not transfer to another diocese or enter a religious congregation.[21]

[19] Prümmer, p. 272; cf. Cappello, *Summa Iuris Canonici* (3 vols., Vols. I-II, 4 ed.; Vol. III, 3. ed., Romae: apud Aedes Universitatis Gregorianae, 1945-1948), II, p. 47, n. 37.

[19a] Cf. McBride, pp. 143-144.

[20] Instr. S. C. de Prop. F., 27 apr. 1871, §10—*Collectanea S. C. P. F.*, II, n. 1369.

[21] *Ibid.*, §13; response of the Sacred Congregation for the Propagation of the Faith, febr. 4, 1873—*Acta et Decreta Concilii Plenarii Baltimorensis Tertii, A. D. MDCCCLXXXIV* (Baltimorae: John Murphy, 1886), Appendix, pp. 209-211.

Even if by special permission he should later enter a religious Order or congregation, then because of the common good the cleric is obliged, in virtue of his oath, to work perpetually for the salvation of souls in the diocese or the vicariate to the service of which he is bound. Without an additional special permission of the Holy See, he cannot enter a religious institute not engaged in missionary work in the respective territory, and if he should enter such an institute he could be dismissed for that reason alone.[22]

From this consideration of the practice of the Church, it is noticed that great emphasis is placed on spiritual good, even to the exclusion of entry into religion if the Holy See should judge that the spiritual necessity of the mission is so great that the cleric cannot be spared. Quite similar is the reason for the restriction in the second part of the impediment of canon 542, 2° *pr.* Although under the "title of the mission" the common good to souls is emphasized in a positive manner, canon 542, 2° *pr.*, contains the same basic idea, although the concept is expressed in a negative manner when the Code guards against grave harm to souls.

As said before, this particular reason of serious spiritual injury resulting to the faithful is the only one which justifies the local ordinary in his opposition to the cleric's permanent departure from his diocese. Any other reasons advanced, e.g., that the cleric is an indispensable secretary, an excellent chauffeur,. or a very capable athletic director, are not in themselves sufficient justifying reasons for it. Neither would a cleric entering the novitiate despite such uncanonical contradiction be admitted illicitly.

Moreover, if it is evident that the local ordinary alleges grave harm to souls as a mere pretext to retain the cleric, the subject would not be bound by the impediment, provided he had previously consulted his ordinary. Whenever there is a prudent doubt as to whether or not the reason alleged by the bishop falls within the scope of this one category, the cleric must comply with the express wish

[22] Cf. McBride, p. 144.

of his bishop. In reference to others the local ordinary is in a position to have a more accurate understanding of the spiritual condition of his diocese and of the number of available priests to accomplish the work of the ministry. However, during the time of his submission to the order of his bishop, the cleric may have recourse to the Holy See.[23]

As a conclusion to the matter presented thus far in this chapter, it is proper to recall that the formal impediment of canon 542, 2° *pr.*, is new in the present canonical legislation. In the past the emphasis and the general practice of the Church has been to protect the freedom of clerics to enter religion. In fact, a cleric was simply not to be prevented from entering religion, but in exceptional cases he might be recalled if his departure from his church had caused serious harm. In the Code, the only difference is that now the cleric can be prevented from entering the religious life when serious spiritual harm to souls is involved. As the general rule of the past was in favor of admittance, so now the same principle stands, except for the positive restriction placed by the Code.[24]

In the light of history, therefore, it can readily be understood in what manner grave harm might result from a cleric's departure, especially a priest's, when he demands his immediate release from the diocese. On the other hand, the writer favors the conclusion that seldom are there to be found such circumstances as will occasion grave harm when a reasonable time for making other arrangements to fill a future vacant office has intervened.[25] Even more rarely would there be verified any conditions sufficient to justify a perpetual refusal. Most infrequently, indeed, would there arise circumstances that could adequately justify the

[23] Larraona, "Commentarium Codicis," *CpRM*, XVII (1936), 245-246.

[24] Can. 6, 2°, 3°.

[25] Cf. Prümmer, p. 272; Schaefer, *De Religiosis*, p. 441, n. 803; Peinador, "Sacerdotium Saeculare et Status Religiosus . . . ," *CpRM*, XX (1939), 326.

retention of a subdeacon or a deacon, and this because of their limited canonical ability to fill important positions in the Church today.

ARTICLE 4. CONSIDERATION OF CIRCUMSTANCES WHICH BRING ABOUT GRAVE, SPIRITUAL HARM UPON A MAJOR CLERIC'S DEPARTURE

A. Small Number of Priests in a Diocese

At times prelates hesitate to acknowledge the presence of a religious vocation in one of their clerical subjects or to allow him to dedicate himself to God through the profession of vows. They falter because of their great responsibility in leading souls safely to God over a perilous and materialistic path, and because they must shoulder this burden with a relatively small number of priests to assist them. It is their first reaction and almost a natural one for them to contend that every priest in their diocese is important in fulfilling the duties of the ecclesiastical ministrations; otherwise the candidates would not have been ordained for their particular dioceses. Yet the Code does not contemplate or justify a general criterion of this kind for the retention of clerical subjects. Each individual case is to be studied carefully and open-mindedly for the gaining of a distinct perception of whether the departure of the given cleric will actually be the occasion of grave harm to souls, a serious harm that cannot by any other arrangement at all be averted. In a diocese with a small number of priests, it is true that there are present certain aggravating conditions which will work together so that a cleric at times is dispensable only at the expense of serious spiritual injury to souls.

Nevertheless, the presentation of certain important considerations will offer some guidance to those who are called upon to decide whether or not a major cleric's going from the diocese will seriously injure the spiritual welfare of souls. In the sixth century, the Emperor Mauritius (582-602) also conceived a fear that his military forces would become very small if so many of his soldiers continued to enter the religious life. Whereupon Pope St. Gergory I, in writing to the Emperor in 589, rebuked him for his anxiety and for the enactment of subsequent legislation that restricted a soldier's freedom to enter a religious institute. To his reproach the Pope added the reason that the strength of the Emperor's army would increase in proportion to the increase in prayer among the members of the army of God in the religious life.[26]

A similar objection against admitting priests too readily into religion was considered by St. Thomas:

> ... What is lawful to one is likewise lawful to all. But if all priests having the care of souls were to enter religion, the people would be left without a pastor's care, which would be unfitting. Therefore it seems that parish priests cannot lawfully enter religion.[26a]

In his reply to this objection, St. Thomas referred to St. Jerome's argument against Vigilantius:

> Although they, namely religious, are sorely smitten by thy poisonous tongue, about whom you argue, saying: 'If all shut themselves up and live in solitude, who will go to church? who will convert worldlings? who will be able to urge sinners to virtue?' If this holds true, if all are fools with thee, who can be wise? Virginity itself will not be commendable, for if all be virgins, and none marry, the human race will perish. Virtue is rare, and is not desired by many.[26b]

This response of St. Jerome St. Thomas adapted in answering the objection that parish priests are admitted too freely into the religious life, and stated: "It is therefore evident that this [fear] is a foolish alarm; thus might a

[26] Ep. 62, lib. 2—Mansi, IX, 1152, 1153.

[26a] *Summa Theologica,* IIa-IIae, q. 189, a. 7. Translation by the English Dominican Province.

[26b] *Contra Vigilantium—Summa Theologica, loc. cit.* Translation by English Dominican Province. St. Jerome's argument can also be found in *MPL,* XXIII, 351.

man fear to draw water lest the river run dry."[26c] The Angelic Doctor pressed his contention by designating as praiseworthy any assistance given others in their purpose of entering religion.[27] Moreover, he allowed the parish priests to fulfill their desire of embracing the religious life without the obligation of consulting many persons and of deliberating a long period of time.

Another worthwhile consideration is the principle that a secular priest upon entrance into a religious institute still retains his sacerdotal character and does not become incapable of rendering priestly service to the diocese.[28] Either the priest himself or a confrere of his in the community usually is available to the diocese when the charge of souls exceeds the time and energy of the secular priesthood. Especially is this verified when the religious house is located in the diocese itself. In fact, the Code itself legislates for the employment of their clerical services. Canon 1334 states that if the local ordinary judges the help of the religious to be necessary for imparting catechetical in-

[26c] *Loc. cit.* Translation by English Dominican Province.

[27] *Summa Theologica,* IIa-IIae, q. 189, a. 9. Translation by English Dominican Province.

[28] Cf. a letter and decree of Pope Siricius (†399) to Bishop Himerius, February 10, 385—JK, n. 255; c. 29, C. XVI, q. 1. That the religious life by its very nature was incompatible with the care of souls and the burdens of pastoral work was the doctrine held by the Synod of Pistoja in 1786. But this teaching was condemned by Pope Pius VI. The exact words of the proposition and its condemnation are as follows: "Regula 1, quae statuit universe, et indiscriminatim *statum regularem, aut monasticum natura sua componi non posse cum animarum cura, cumque vitae pastoralis muneribus, nec adeo in partem venire posse ecclesiasticae hierarchiae, quin ex adverso pugnet cum ipsiusmet vitae monasticae principiis,*

"*Falsa, perniciosa, in sanctissimos Ecclesiae patres, et praesules, qui regularis vitae instituta cum clericalis ordinis muneribus consciarunt, iniuriosa, pio, vetusto, probato Ecclesiae mori, Summorumque Pontificum sanctionibus contraria*: quasi monachi quos morum gravitas, et vitae, ac fidei institutio sancta commendat, *non rite, nec modo sine religionis offensione,* sed et *cum multa utilitate Ecclesiae* clericorum officiis *aggregentur.*"—Pius VI, const. *Auctorem fidei,* 28 aug. 1794, prop. Synodi Pistorien. damn. LXXX—*Fontes,* n. 475.

struction to his people, the religious, though exempt, are obliged upon request of the ordinary to give such instructions, either in person or through their subjects, especially in their own churches. The only mentioned exception which excuses the religious from this obligation is resultant detriment to religious discipline.

Church law determines the norm which the local ordinary is to follow in regard to delegated jurisdiction given the religious for the hearing of confessions. The ordinary is not permitted habitually to grant the faculties for the hearing of confessions to religious who have not been presented to him by the superior, nor without a serious reason is he permitted to refuse faculties to him who is presented by his proper religious superior.[29]

Moreover a local ordinary shall not without grave cause refuse the faculty of preaching to those religious who are presented by their proper superior, nor without a grave reason recall the faculty once granted, especially not from all the priests of a community at one and the same time.[30] This implies of course that the religious priest possesses a reputation for good moral conduct and sufficient knowledge as ascertained by previous examination.[31] The possibility of religious clerics cooperating with the diocesan clergy in the Church's care for souls is further demonstrated by legislative references to religious parishes and benefices,[32] the appointment of religious to such offices and their removal therefrom,[33] and the financial administration of parochial funds.[34] Additional legislation devoted entirely to the obligations and privileges of religious promoted to an ecclesiastical dignity or to the charge of a parish is found in the thirteenth title of the second book of the Code.

All of the foregoing canonical legislation emphasizes the fitness of a religious priest for the performance of such ministerial functions as are demanded for the good of individual

[29] Can. 874; cf. can. 877.

[30] Can. 1339, §1.

[31] Can. 1340; cf. 877.

[32] Can. 1411, n. 2; can. 1430, §1.

[33] Canons 1442; 454, §5; 2157, §2.

[34] Canons 533, §1, 4°; 535, §3, 2°.

souls and the Church in general. Moreover, the rights and duties of religious and local ordinaries are thus clearly determined, so that each, knowing what is demanded by the Church, may give his complete cooperation to the one great work of saving souls. Such reverential coordination and charitable harmony among the diocesan and religious clergy can only redound to the greater flourishing of peace and the apostolate in Christ's vineyard.[35]

Further, to establish the compatibility between the religious state and pastoral administration, it is worthy of note that the Roman Pontiffs have, in particular cases, urged that former secular clerics who had embraced the religious life should return as religious to their diocese to assist in parochial work. In fact, it was under a similar condition that the alumni of a German college were allowed entry to the religious life.[36]

The foregoing review of the conviction of Pope St. Gregory I, of the doctrine proposed by St. Thomas, and of the juridical recognition of the compatibility of the religious priesthood with the performance of pastoral functions has offered considerations which cannot be lightly brushed aside when a clerical subject consults his ordinary concerning his future entrance into religion. These facts are relevant not only in large and long established dioceses, but also in small and recently erected dioceses.

To the above-mentioned reasons demonstrating why a bishop should act carefully and cautiously when he thinks himself justified in opposing his cleric's entry into religion, a stronger reason can be added. This reason derives from the fact that the practice of the Church has never been an enhancement of the number of the secular clergy through any process of secularization on the part of religious. If the Church, therefore, does not approve of secularization of religious as a means for increasing a small number of

[35] Cf. Clemens X, const. *Superna*, 21 iun. 1670—*Fontes*, n. 246.

[36] "... statim ad juvandas animas revertantur in patriam."—Julius Cordara, *Historia Collegii Germanici et Hungarici* (Romae, 1770), lib. 4, n. 28, p. 172, as quoted by Nilles, *Selectae Disputationes*, p. 90.

priests in a given diocese, is it not logical to say that the Church also disapproves the stifling of a religious vocation as an efficient and habitual device to increase the number of the diocesan clergy?

By secularization is meant the accepted permission to leave the religious institute permanently. It is, therefore, a total permanent release from the religious life, granted at the behest of a religious who wants to return to the world for good. The Holy See alone can grant an indult to a member of a pontifical institute, while the bishop can grant it to a member of a diocesan institute lawfully residing in his territory.[37] For the safeguarding of religious discipline, serious reasons must be presented to the respective superior granting the indult. He in turn will not concede the permission without previously obtaining necessary information from the subject's superior as well as his appraisal (*votum*) concerning the merits of the case. Sufficient reasons for the requesting of an indult of secularization are bad health, mental disposition, and assistance required by the parents of the religious.[38]

The effects of secularization upon a religious who has accepted the indult and has left the institute are: a) he is separated from his institute; he must put off the religious garb and conduct himself as a secular in all things concerning the celebration of Mass, the recitation of the canonical hours, the use and administration of the sacraments; b) he is freed from his vows, retaining however the obligations connected with major orders, but he is no longer obliged to recite the divine office by reason of his previous profession, nor is he bound by the other rules of the relinquished institute; c) he must repeat his novitiate and profession and take his rank among the professed as from the day of his new profession if later through an apostolic indult he should again be received into the novitiate.[39] A

[37] Can. 638.

[38] Schaefer, *De Religiosis*, p. 917, n. 1538.

[39] Can. 640.

religious in sacred orders who has lost his proper diocese and now has become secularized may not exercise his sacred orders until he has found a bishop willing to receive him, or the Holy See has made other provisions.[40] Other disabilities of a secularized religious are that he is forbidden to obtain the following benefices and offices without a new and special indult from the Holy See: a) any benefice in a major and minor basilica or in a cathedral church; b) any professorship or office in a major or minor seminary, or in a college in which clerics are educated, or in a university or institute enjoying an apostolic privilege for the granting of academic degrees; c) any office or position in a diocesan curia, or in a religious house, whether of men or women religious, even in a congregation of merely diocesan approval.[41] Neither may the secularized religious demand any financial remuneration for services rendered to the institute.[42]

The weighty reasons demanded for the obtaining of an indult of secularization, the complete breaking of every bond with the religious community so highly appreciated by each member, the disagreeable effects and the canonical disabilities for a number of diocesan clerical positions, emphasize a certain displeasure and distaste that the Church feels in allowing a person to abandon the religious state of perfection. If the Church treats cautiously and even severely those who forsake the pursuit of religious perfection through secularization, therein can be found a definite standard by which to judge its zeal for the preservation of and continuance in a religious vocation.

Since the Church evidently frowns upon the idea of secularization, it is impossible to imagine that the Church would allow it as a means for swelling the number of the diocesan clergy. Peinador, a noted writer on the comparison of the perfection of the priesthood with the perfection of the religious state, maintains that not even a most serious need of priestly workers in a diocese would demand the secularization of religious priests, since the religious state

[40] Can. 641. [41] Can. 642, §1. [42] Can. 643, §1.

is compatible with the pastoral ministry.[43] A serious need of spiritual ministration to souls in a diocese, although this necessity, as equivalent to grave harm to God's children, might prevent a cleric's departure from his charge, is never a legitimate cause for a complete departure from the religious life. In addition, the same writer recalls that, while history testifies to the dissolution of certain religious Orders, the reason of supplying more priests for the diocese was never advanced in vindication of such a far-reaching exercise of authority.[44] Through the centuries members of various religious institutes have been actively engaged in the instruction of the faithful, but never has the proposition been sustained that an abundance of the spiritual harvest and the fewness of laborers in the Lord's vineyard should compel religious missionaries to avail themselves of the procedure of secularization.[45]

As a deduction from the foregoing, it is impossible to conceive that the Church in view of pastoral needs would generally permit the frustration of a religious vocation, not only after one's actual admittance into a religious institute, but also before one's reception. If the Church is eager to protect a religious vocation subsequent to the profession of vows, it can only lead one to believe that it is equally zealous to safeguard a religious vocation antecedent to the profession of vows. Therefore, as a general principle, the Church is opposed to any unrestricted policy of retaining in a diocese a cleric who has received a divine call to the religious state of perfection. To contradict such a cleric on the ground of the one, justifiable, canonical reason—grave harm to souls which in no other way can be avoided—should rather be looked upon as the unusual thing,

[43] "Sacerdotium Saeculare et Status Religiosus seu de Perfectione comparata inter Sacerdotium Saeculare et Statum Religiosorum," *CpRM*, XX (1939), 325.

[44] *Ibid.*, note 179.

[45] Cf. Pius X, ep. *Approbatio in Perpetuum Constitutionum Congregationis Canonicorum Regularium Immaculatae Conceptionis*, 11 febr. 1913—*AAS*, V (1913), 119.

the exceptional case. It is not easy to conceive that this exceptional instance should become the general practice. The mind of the Church is not that entry to religion should be denied to all clerics, not even during a time when additional priests in a diocese could advantageously be employed in the care of souls. Only a particular and real need of a certain priest on account of his special qualities or exceptional ability can ordinarily give rise to that degree of spiritual grave harm that is contemplated in the Code. In a small or recently established diocese, the departure of any priest regardless of any special talents might easily enough cause such conditions that by his absence some souls would suffer seriously from lack of attention. But the reason itself of the smallness and newness of a diocese is not accepted by the legislator.

The bishop of a small diocese, or as a matter of fact of any diocese, has little reason to fear that the increase of religious vocations within his diocese will be prejudicial to his flock. According to Peinador, an increase of the number of candidates to the religious life will necessarily be the occasion of an increase of the number of secular clerical candidates, since in such a community or diocese a deep and lively faith is fostered, which is fertile in producing vocations to the diocesan priesthood. Peinador argues in the following manner: clerical vocations are numerous in those places where Christian piety is great. But such Christian piety is ardent in places where schools are taught by religious and where they cooperate harmoniously and effectively with the secular clergy. Therefore a greater number of clerical candidates can be expected from such communities or dioceses.[46]

In considering the attitude of the Roman Pontiffs towards the need of more priests, it is found that they do not stress a preference for the secular priesthood at the expense of the priesthood in the religious life. If in their letters and public exhortations the Popes have deplored the

[46] *Ibid.*, p. 326, note 182.

small number of secular clerical vocations, they have never blamed the great number of religious vocations for this deficiency. On the other hand, the Popes have been most zealous in safeguarding the freedom of a cleric to embrace the religious state of perfection if he feels that he has a vocation.[47]

In his encyclical letter on the Catholic priesthood, Pope Pius XI (1922-1939) treated briefly a topic similar to the one under discussion in this article. While the present writer contends that a small number of priests in a diocese is in itself not a sufficient reason for opposing a cleric's entrance into religion, the Pope warned against that false fear of too few priests which prompts the ordaining of unfit and unworthy candidates to the priesthood. The Pope referred to the Angelic Doctor, who long ago answered this difficulty with his usual lucidity:

> God never abandons His Church; and so the number of priests will be always sufficient for the needs of the faithful, provided the worthy are advanced and the unworthy are sent away. Should it ever become impossible to maintain the present number, it is better to have a few good priests than a multitude of bad ones.[48]

Pius XI reaffirmed that one well trained priest is worth more than many priests trained badly or scarcely at all.[49]

It is quite true that specifically the Pope was demanding of bishops and religious superiors a needful caution to preclude the ordaining of ill-trained and unworthy candidates. But is the interpretation too wide if this warning is extended to the retention in the diocese of clerics who have a religious vocation? The person who has received the grace of a call to the state of perfection, but does not follow the same vocation, will surely find the work of his personal salvation more difficult. And if a cleric should

[47] Cf. Peinador, *ibid.*, pp. 326, 327.

[48] *Summa Theologica*, Supplem., q. 36, a. 4, ad 1m. Translation by the writer.

[49] Ep. encycl. *Ad catholici sacerdotii*, 20 dec. 1935—*AAS*, XXVIII (1936), 44.

desire to enter a religious institute for the sake of greater spiritual security and the avoidance of occasions of sin proximate to him, his life in the world will be very difficult, if not despairingly so. In cases of this kind, the cleric might easily turn out to be an unworthy priest against the training of whom the Pope has sounded his warning. Just as false fear of too few priests would prompt the ordaining of candidates who do not measure up to the high standards invoked by the Church, so too a questionable fear might suggest the retention of a cleric in a diocese for the sole reason that there are too few priests in the territory. Yet, when the cleric's departure would cause serious spiritual harm which could not by any other arrangement be averted, the bishop is justified in retaining his cleric in the service of the diocese for the time that conditions remain the same. In his obedience to his bishop who exercises his right in this manner, the cleric will certainly know that for him it is God's will that he remain in the diocese, and that he will receive sufficient divine assistance to comply with God's designs in his regard.

In concluding the discussion of the reason based on the small number of priests in a diocese as possibly justifying the detention of a cleric in the diocese, one may advantageously recall the following principal arguments. The conviction of Pope St. Gregory I, the argumentation of St. Thomas, and the juridical recognition of the compatibility of the priesthood in the religious state with reference to pastoral functions are reasons which do not justify a scarcity of priests as a canonical motive for contradicting a cleric who wants to embrace the religious life. The fact that the Church does not approve of secularization as a method by which to increase the number of diocesan clergy indicates that its attitude in regard to entrance into religion is not marked by any prevention of the initial steps in the pursuit of a religious vocation even in a diocese where priests are few. As Pius XI called the fear of too few priests a false one and warned that it should not serve as a cause for ordaining unfit candidates to the priesthood, so also that same fear of too few priests is false when a cleric is kept in a diocese contrary to the prescriptions of canon 542, 2° *pr.* The fact that the number of priests in a diocese is small does not, in itself, offer a canonical reason for opposing a cleric's entry into the religious life. His departure, however, from such a diocese, in contradistinction to a cleric's leaving a diocese with a relatively large number of priests, can more readily create conditions which would fulfill the prescriptions enacted in canon 542, 2° *pr.*, in virtue of which a bishop is justified in keeping the cleric in the diocese for the time during which the adverse circumstances there remain unchanged.

B. Expenses Incurred by the Seminary for the Free Education of Clerics

Whenever grave harm comes upon souls as a result of a major cleric's departure from a diocese to enter religion, the local ordinary has the canonical right to oppose his admission to the novitiate. Through such opposition the bishop interjects a condition which renders illicit the admission of this cleric into religion. At first glance it would appear that the local ordinary could advance, at least indirectly, the plea of grave spiritual harm to his people whenever one of his clerical subjects who has received free room, board and tuition in the seminary seeks to enter the religious life. Gratuitous education of this kind certainly is not uncommon in many dioceses, while in other dioceses the seminarians are asked to pay at least a part of the expense paid out for their education. Such free education sometimes may give rise to a delicate problem when the recipient desires to change his ordinational title of "service to the diocese" for such other titles as that of "poverty" or of the "common table."[50] The question, therefore, can be formulated as follows: may the bishop oppose a cleric's entrance into a religious institute in a case in which the cleric has received a gratuitous education at

[50] Cf. can. 982.

the expense of the diocese? It is taken for granted that the bishop would base his opposition on the principle that the cleric by his departure will occasion grave harm to souls unless he reimbursed the diocesan seminary fund.

Upon consultation of commentators on the Code, it is found that the authors are generally agreed on the principle that a cleric still possesses full liberty to embrace the religious life, although he has been gratuitously educated and supported in a secular seminary. Although the cleric has not previously reimbursed the diocese, he cannot for that reason itself be opposed on the ground of causing grave harm to souls in a diocese. The authors emphasize the cleric's liberty to enter religion while almost completely ignoring the factor of the free education and support given him in the seminary. Much less do the authors mention or even advert to the presented possibility that the accepted gratuity should form a basis on which to construct an impediment against licit admission into religion.[51]

[51] Larraona, "Commentarium Codicis," *CpRM*, XVII (1936), 244; Schaefer, De Religiosis, p. 441, n. 803: "Ex alia ratione . . . Ordinarius loci ingressum prohibere aut ab eo arcere nequit, etsi Clerici ipsi bonis Seminarii vel Dioecesis sustentati et educati sint." Vermeersch-Creusen, *Epitome,* I, 503, n. 680; Cappello, *Summa Iuris Canonici,* II, p. 48, n. 37: "Ratio sufficiens prohibendi ingressum in religionem non et factum quod clericus expensis dioecesis educatus fuerit in Seminario, licet forte accesserit promissio etiam iurata indemne faciendi Seminarium;" Beste, ad can. 542, 2°: "Clerico qui statum religiosum amplecti cogitat, nequit per se imponi obligatio compensandi sumptus a dioecesi in ipso alendo et educando factos, multoque minus poterit ei ingressus in religionem ob eiusmodi dispendia impedire, nisi is speciali pacto aut conditione ultro citroque acceptata expresse se obligaverit ad has expensas resarciendas;" Woywod, "Seminarians Entering Religious Community and Compensation to Diocese for Expenses Incurred," *The Homiletic and Pastoral Review* (New York: Wagner, 1900—), XXIX (1929), 996-998: "The law does not in the least refer to the expenses borne by the diocese in the education of the clerics, but simply declares that, with the exceptions mentioned, they are free to join a religious community. The Church educates the boys and young men in the minor and major seminaries at the expense of the diocese in the hope that they, having declared their intention to study for the priesthood, will persevere and in the

Vermeersch-Creusen offer a weighty reason for their own stand when they refer to the Sacred Congregation of the Council's demand to delete a provision in the synodal statutes of an Italian diocese which required of secular clerics, upon their entrance into the religious life, the reimbursing of the diocese for the free education they had received.[52] To see more clearly the extent of the difficulties and complications involved, it is necessary that a few more basic principles be recalled in regard to the establishment of a seminary and its functions.

The Council of Trent legislated for the erection of a diocesan or provincial seminary to assume the work of training clerics for all the churches of the diocese to take the place of the plan under which each church was obliged to train its own. Such a seminary was always, according to the tenor of the decree, to be a place of free education except for those who were rich enough to pay for themselves.[53] To make funds available for the carrying out of this legislation, the Council imposed a strict tax on all benefices and ecclesiastical revenues of various kinds to aid in forming in each diocese the seminary's administrative

course of time serve the Church. If the young men believe themselves called to the religious life and want to follow the call, they are not abandoning the service of the Church, but rather devote themselves to it in a more perfect way. For this reason the S. C. C. (Feb. 26, 1695) declared that no compensation can be demanded by the diocese for expenses incurred, when a student studying at the expense of the diocese enters a religious community."

[52] *Epitome, loc. cit.*: "Minus etiam obstat si seminarium, in alendo clerico, sumptus aliquos fecerit. Nisi enim, conceptis verbis, in ipsa census (bursae) constitutione aliter et legitime cautum fuerit, seminarista communi iure regitur; iure autem illo ingressus permittitur . . . S. C. C., 26 febr. 1695—Nec per se, qui inter studia ad propositum capessendae religionis devenerit, id episcopo vel Superioribus manifestare debet. Namque haec est ex iure communi sminaristarum condicio, ut publicis impendiis instituatur; et tamen, ex eodem iure, integrum ipsis est religionem ingredi."

[53] Sess. XXIII, *de ref.*, c. 18: "Pauperum autem filios praecipue eligi vult; nec tamen ditiorum excludit; modo suo sumptu alantur, et studium prae se ferant Deo, et ecclesiae inserviendi."

fund. Canon 1355, which refers to the Tridentine law in the footnote, contains similar legislation applicable when pecuniary resources are wanting for the building and maintenance of the seminary, and the support of students. It permits the bishop to order the pastors and rectors of churches (even the exempt ones) to take up at stated times a collection in their churches for that purpose and to impose a seminary tax in his diocese. If these means are not sufficient, he may annex some simple benefices to the seminary.

In commenting on the establishment and support of seminaries as determined in the Council of Trent and on the possible restitution of the expenses incurred for the free education received, McBride observed that, as long as a poor student had the right intention upon entering the seminary, he could not be prevented, on the ground of gratuitous education at least, from leaving the service of the diocese for an honorable reason, either during or after his seminary career. Neither could he be compelled to reimburse the seminary, since he did not violate any law. However, if he was of wealthy parents and received his seminary education gratuitously, he could be forced to restore its cost, for the Council of Trent did not command the dioceses to educate such students;[54] so also, even if he was poor, but at the same time lacked the intention of persevering, he could be bound in justice to reimburse the diocese.[55]

Except for the two latter exceptions mentioned, there can be found nothing in the Council of Trent or in the twenty-first title of the third book of the Code concerning seminaries, which would imply that the diocese has a strict claim on a cleric gratuitously educated in its seminary. There is no reference to an obligation which would demand of a

[54] Monacelli, *Formularium Legale, Practicum* (3 vols., Venetiis, 1736-1751), tom. II, tit. XIII, form. 7, n. 19.

[55] McBride, pp. 178-180.

cleric that he either serve the diocese perpetually or reimburse it should he enter religion.[56]

Besides the manner of supporting a seminary as outlined by the Council of Trent, Nilles took note of the fact that it can also be supported by some other religious fund or estate, as in Austria, or by certain civil taxes and contributions, as in France, or from manual donations from the faithful. Yet, no matter by which method seminaries are supported in reality, the support is always derived from ecclesiastical funds, i.e., from goods destined to meet the needs of the Church. With reference to such public ecclesiastical seminaries in which clerics are publicly educated, so the same writer continues, the question was asked whether these same clerics must reimburse the diocese when they wish to embrace the religious life. Nilles maintained that the clerics in such cases should not be held to an obligation which cannot be proved by law. He further contended that the necessity of repayment in such particular cases could not be found stated in any legislation, and the Roman Pontiffs had repeatedly asserted the freedom of clerics to enter religion without making any mention of reimbursement to the diocese.[57]

The same author made the statement, with which the present writer agrees, that there cannot be demanded a remuneration for the gratuitous education when a cleric desires to join a religious community. Such a demand for

[56] The possibility, though, does exist that the donor of a burse might have attached some restrictions against complete freedom to enter religion as considered in relation to the consumption of a gratuity. Such possible restriction will be discussed later, pp. 146-150.

[57] In fact, Nilles held that not even the wealthy seminarians educated freely in seminaries erected according to the mind of the Council of Trent would be bound to pay the expenses paid out for their education when abandoning the clerical life.—*Selectae Disputationes*, p. 102. The present writer finds it difficult to agree with that opinion, for the Tridentine legislation did single out the poor as the beneficiaries of these seminaries. If wealthy students desired to study for the priesthood, they were expected to pay from their own wealth for their support and education in the same seminary.

repayment can hardly be reconciled with the Church's legislation in protecting the cleric's freedom. Should reimbursement of this kind be said to be due in justice, one would be forced to conclude that consequently the cleric's liberty to enter religion has been greatly restricted, almost limited, so that a mere and empty vestige of liberty would remain. In the majority of cases, poorer clerics would be unable to repay the amount expended for their education and support in the minor and major seminary. Considering the excellence of the religious state of perfection and also the famous letter of Pope Benedict XIV, one must seek not to weaken and unnecessarily limit the cleric's liberty to enter a religious institute, but rather to safeguard and confirm that freedom. Any undue restriction would hardly be in harmony with the principles of liberty to enter religion, which principles were so universally applied throughout history.[58]

The extrinsic arguments based on the common opinion of many authors, the legislation of the Council of Trent, and the intrinsic argument connected with the Holy See's action against a synodal statute in Cesena, Italy, are arguments which point to a solution of the question proposed at the beginning of this discussion. They are reasons which force the conclusion that ordinarily no repayment can be demanded from a cleric who has been educated at the expense of the diocese, when he afterwards expresses his intention of embracing the religious life.[59] Neither can the lack of remuneration be held to be equivalent to a cause effecting grave spiritual harm to souls in the diocese.

The problem of reimbursement was discussed merely for the sake of a solution to the question asked previously. The exoneration of the cleric in regard to any reimbursement

[58] Cf. Nilles, *op. cit.*, pp. 103-104.

[59] It is taken for granted that this change of intention was not contemplated secretly by the cleric during his stay at the secular seminary. Such secrecy is not likely to happen if the bishop frequently visits the seminary to obtain reports on dispositions, vocations, etc., of the seminarians, as outlined in canon 1357, §2.

before his entry into religion does not in any way prove that a debt was actually contracted in the first place. As far as the writer is concerned, that problem is still unanswered, and has no place in this study. But should there be the contraction of a real debt which consequently demanded repayment, that financial obligation would not form a part of the first impediment of canon 542, 2°, but rather it would belong to the second, i.e., that they who are burdened with debts and remain unable to settle their obligations are illicitly admitted into the novitiate.

In concluding this discussion, one will admit that a diocese which has freely or at a reduced rate educated and supported a seminarian does appear, from a factual human point of view, to suffer a total financial loss when a cleric separates himself from that diocese to embrace the religious life. In regard to the pecuniary resources involved, it cannot be denied that several thousand dollars spent on a seminarian will produce little, if any, return in service to the diocese. Nevertheless, this disagreeable financial condition is not in itself a sufficient reason for judging that a grave spiritual harm is occasioned for souls. Here two entirely different considerations and values are concerned, the one an apparent financial loss to the diocese, the other a grave spiritual harm to souls. Yet it is not impossible that the one might affect the other. Although an extreme case, the following instance will portray what is meant. Take a small and poor diocese in which a pastor of a parish consults his bishop about the future entrance into a religious community. The bishop would gladly release the pastor for the pursuing of his noble purpose, but is forced to refuse the request on the ground that he cannot get another priest to take care of the parish. Whereupon the pastor offers to pay all expenses incurred by the diocese in his education. With this reimbursement, the pastor suggests that another priest, secular or religious, could be obtained from the neighboring diocese, at least for the period of time needed by the bishop till he can fill the vacancy with one of his own priests. As is evident, in such a case there is a close reaction between the financial sum involved, on the one hand, and the grave spiritual harm to souls, on the other. Yet, the financial loss itself which the diocese sustains cannot be adduced, and is not so advanced in this supposition, as a canonical reason for opposing a cleric's entry into a religious institute. This payment is made only to remove the local ordinary's justified refusal by assisting him financially to get additional help for the diocese and thus to avert the serious harm which the bishop foresees.

Prescinding from an unusual case such as the one just considered, the writer answers to the question proposed at the beginning of this discussion that the local ordinary may not rightly contradict the entrance into religion of a cleric who has received a gratuitous education at the expense of the diocese.

C. Possible Restrictions on the Use of Gratuities as Specified in the Establishment of a Burse or Fund

Donors of a fund or founders of a burse for the supplying of gratuitous education of clerics have the right to attach to their largess certain conditions not opposed directly or indirectly to the law of the Church. For instance, if a benefactor wished to help priests for a particular diocese, he could make it effective by a prior condition that any student accepting the benefits be bound to remain in the diocese or repay the amount spent on his training if he returned to the lay state.[60] If a party accepts a gratuity under such terms, he enters a contract binding him in justice.[61]

[60] History records two cases in which founders had placed such conditions against a cleric's return to the lay state; the Sacred Congregation of the Council did not interfere.—*Tiburtina,* 11 mart. 1752, and *Ferrarien.,* 20 ian. 1821—Angelus Lucidi, *De Visitatione Sacrorum Liminum* (3. ed., 3 vols., Romae, 1883), II, 356-357. Of course the cleric's complete liberty in receiving orders must be safeguarded. He should not be frightened with the possibility of a huge debt upon him if he should decide that he really has no vocation to the priesthood.

[61] McBride, p. 183.

At this point, one may well recall briefly the present legislation concerning pious foundations. Canon 1544 gives the definition of a pious foundation and also indicates the obligation incurred by the recipient. By the term, pious foundation, is meant the grant of temporal goods to some ecclesiastical moral person in any manner with the obligation to say certain Masses, or perform other specified ecclesiastical functions, or execute some works of piety or charity perpetually or for a long period of time in return for the income derived from the endowment. The foundation, when legitimately accepted, has the nature of a bilateral contract, *do ut facias,* binding both parties.[62]

A pious foundation given to the seminary for the training of candidates to the secular priesthood might contain such licit conditions as the following: a) that a cleric in the diocesan seminary may no longer partake of the free support and education resulting from the foundation once he has firmly determined to embrace the religious life; b) that the cleric be bound to make known to his proper bishop or the rector of the seminary his intention of following a religious vocation.[63] With reservations of this sort, only students destined for the secular clergy would take advantage of the gratuitous education and support, while at the same time the seminarians would possess complete freedom to join the religious life. And if a seminarian, studying under these conditions, though fully intent upon future entrance to the religious life, deliberately refused to inform his bishop or the rector of the seminary, such a cleric made himself guilty of breaking his part of the contract and consequently of a serious wrong.[64]

[62] Cf. canon 1362, which refers to the income from legacies given to a seminary and the possibility of restrictions added thereto.

[63] Cf. Vermeersch-Creusen, *Epitome,* I, 503, n. 680; Cocchi, *Commentarium in Codicem,* Vol. IV, n. 64, p. 136.

[64] St. Charles Borromeo (1538-1584) in the erection of his seminary ruled thus: "Unusquisque sit ea mente ac voluntate, ut omnino velit in bonum ministrum pro hujus ecclesiae Mediolanensis adjumento evadere... Quod si quis decursu temporis de statu mutando consilium caperet, etiamsi de religione ingredienda cogitaret, de eo reverendissi-

There is another condition, however, concerning which authors are not in complete agreement as to its legality. The difficulty is this: is the founder of a burse or a donor justified in forestalling entry into religion by demanding repayment of that amount consumed in the seminary? Previous to any statement regarding the diverse opinions, mention should be made of the fact that in commenting on canon 542, 2° *pr.*, many noted canonists, among them Berutti,[65] Blat,[66] Coronata,[67] De Meester,[68] Fanfani,[69] Prümmer,[70] Regatillo,[71] Schaefer,[72] and Wernz-Vidal[73] do not take into account the possibility of such a condition attached to a burse, or the effect it would have upon a major cleric seeking admission into the religious life.

For the affirmative opinion there is Beste, who makes the general statement, as do many of the authors, that the obligation of compensation to the diocese for the amount consumed in the cleric's support and education cannot absolutely be imposed upon the cleric; much less can his entry into religion be prohibited on this account. But Beste goes a step further when he says that these two prohibitions can be allowed if the cleric has expressly obligated himself by

mum archiepiscopum vel rectorem statim certiorem faciat. Peccaret enim, si in seminario hoc animo viveret, in alium finem consumens, quod ad operarios solum pro hujus ecclesiae auxilio sustentandos est constitutum."—*Institutiones Seminarii*, pars III, cap. 1, §*fin.*, as quoted by Nilles, *Selectae Disputationes*, p. 112.

[65] *Institutiones Iuris Canonici,* III, 144.

[66] *Commentarium Textus Codicis,* II *De Personis,* pars II, n. 298, pp. 285-286.

[67] *Institutiones Iuris Canonici,* I, p. 713, n. 571.

[68] *Juris Canonici et Juris Canonico-civilis Compendium,* II, p. 432, n. 992.

[69] Ludovicus Fanfani, *De Iure Religiosorum ad Normam Codicis Iuris Canonici* (2 ed., Taurini-Romae: Marietti, 1925), p. 200, n. 180.

[70] *Manuale Iuris Canonici,* p. 272, n. 205.

[71] *Institutiones Iuris Canonici,* I, p. 387, n. 693.

[72] *De Religiosis,* 440-441, n. 802-803.

[73] *Ius Canonicum,* III, p. 207, n. 254.

a special pact or in consequence of the prescriptions of such a clause to offer remuneration.[74]

For the negative opinion, there is the statement of Cappello who, although he does not discuss the exact difficulty as indicated above, does hold that even a sworn promise to repay the seminary would not be a sufficient reason to impede entry into a religious institute by a cleric who has not paid the "owed" amount.[75] However, Cappello offers no reason for this statement.

Another author for the negative side is Nilles, who designated such a condition as unfair and unworthy of a donor. To him the condition seemed to be unfair inasmuch as by the required payment the cleric whom God has called to the religious life is treated harshly, while the cleric not so called is freed from any obligation of paying for his seminary education. To Nilles the condition appeared as reflecting disgrace upon the donor for the reason that the act of gratuity thus implemented would frequently have prevented a cleric from pursuing a religious vocation, and even in some cases would have impeded the cleric from the use of such means of salvation as were necessary for him in his particular difficulty and temptations.[76]

But the most weighty argument for the negative opinion is the fact that the Holy See has not allowed local ordinaries to enact legislation which would prevent clerics from embracing the religious life before they had reimbursed the diocese with the amount expended for their free education and support.[77] By this direct intervention of the Holy See, the mind of the legislator is clearly indicated in regard to the compensation demanded by the local ordinary. There-

[74] "Clerico, qui statum religiosum amplecti cogitat, nequit per se imponi obligatio compensandi sumptus a dioecesi in ipso alendo et educando factos, multoque minus poterit ei ingressus in religionem ob eiusmodi dispendia impedire, nisi is speciali pacto aut conditione ultor citroque acceptata expresse se obligaverit ad has expensas resarciendas."—*Introductio in Codicem,* ad can. 542, 2°.

[75] *Summa Iuris Canonici,* II, p. 47, note 11.

[76] *Selectae Disputationes,* p. 105.

[77] *Infra,* p. 151.

fore, in an analogous case as regards compensation as a condition attached to a burse, it can be said that the Holy See would equally disapprove of such a restriction on the liberty of clerics. The writer consequently holds with Cappello and Nilles that such a condition may not licitly be added to the founding of a burse or the granting of a donation.[78] It is very difficult, indeed, to justify the acceptance of a burse which requires reimbursement from a cleric who wants to enter the religious state after he has received several years of free training in a diocesan seminary.[79]

Finally, any justifiable restriction on the use of a gratuity as specified in the foundation of a burse demands in itself that both parties to the contract fulfill their obligations. Unless a cleric's violation of such conditions, however, causes that injury to souls referred to in canon 542, 2° *pr.*, his continued service in the diocese cannot be demanded on that score alone. Such infidelity on the part of the cleric undoubtedly would be brought to light in the issuing of testimonial letters to be sent to the religious superior.[80]

D. Possible Restrictions in Synodal Legislation against Entry into a Religious Institute by a Cleric

May a bishop in his synodal statutes decree that any student who receives a free education in his seminary will

[78] What obligations would result from the fact that a local ordinary has accepted a bond from a seminarian who afterwards intends to transfer to the religious life? Such an agreement surely would not be sufficient for opposition by the local ordinary to the cleric's entry into religion according to the norm of canon 542, 2° *pr.* An arrangement of this nature might fall within the scope of the second impediment listed under canon 542, 2°, that is the one concerning grave debts.

[79] If such a burse has been accepted, the fact itself does not justify the local ordinary's denial of his clerical subject's intention to transfer to the religious life according to canon 542, 2° *pr.* The writer hardly questions its validity; therefore he contends that it would be regulated by the second impediment listed under canon 542, 2°, i. e., on grave debts.

[80] Cf. can. 544, §4.

be bound to make repayment if he should later on decide to enter the religious life? The answer to this question is found partly in the fact that a cleric who thus leaves the diocese wherein he was educated does not actually abandon the clerical state, but rather binds himself more strictly thereto. It cannot be denied that every person has the right to strive for perfection. If it can be questioned as to whether every person, lay as well as clerical, has a strict right to seek this perfection in the religious state of perfection, it cannot be doubted, much less denied, that the Church has always respected his liberty to do so. The Holy See has repeatedly insisted on that liberty despite financial obligations, if they can be called such, towards reimbursing the seminary for the gratuitous education received there.

It is of particular interest to note that the synodal statutes of Cesena, Italy, had demanded the reimbursement of the seminary fund by a cleric who wanted to leave the ranks of the secular clergy either to return to the lay state or to embrace the religious life. But the Sacred Congregation, on February 26, 1695, ordered that the clause restricting the freedom of entering religion be omitted.[81] Thereby the Sacred Congregation indicated that this required payment towards the diocesan seminary fund is against the mind of the Church when the cleric desires to enter religion.

Another example of similar episcopal legislation was made in 1882 by a certain bishop of Bavaria. He ruled that he would not ordain to the priesthood any cleric who would not previously oblige himself in writing: 1) to work in the service of the diocese for at least six years; and 2) to restore to the diocese the expenses incurred by his education (ca. 2000 marks) in case he wished to leave for any reason whatever after the completion of the six years. However, four deacons refused to sign these promises and appealed to Pope Leo XIII. Through the Sacred Congrega-

[81] Monacelli, *Formularium Legale*, supplement to tom. II, n. 108.

tion for Extraordinary Affairs, the Pope settled their case by having them ask their bishop once more for ordination to the priesthood while at the same time they were to promise filial submission, obedience and perpetual service to the diocese as long as it was not God's will at some time to call them to a state of greater perfection.[82]

From the two instances cited, it is evident that the Church is opposed to diocesan statutes exacting from a secular cleric the reimbursement or even the promise of reimbursement to the seminary for the gratuitous education received there, in case the cleric wanted to enter the religious life.

Looking once more at what the learned Jesuit author, Nilles, had to say about synodal statutes of this kind, one finds that he regarded them as unreasonable and unjust. For if a restriction of this kind were permitted in a particular instance, that clerical liberty which the sacred canons of the Church have always guarded so carefully would soon be destroyed radically. Furthermore, if clerics were bound to the observance of such a forced promise, they frequently could not enter the religious life, and thus the prohibition might sometimes deprive them from the use of the spiritual means necessary for their own salvation.[83]

In any event, the Council of Trent determined the manner of establishing a seminary and of supporting the students. Fundamentally this legislation is the same in the present legislation. If any single bishop by his own authority could set up conditions for admission contrary to those of the Council, the common law of the Church would soon be overthrown. Any derogation, and even more, any abrogation, of a general law of the Church pertains to the Supreme

[82] "Voluntas est Smi Patris, ut quatuor diaconi scribant proprio ordinario exprimentes sensus filiales obsequii, implorantes gratiam ordinationis, . . . promittentes fideles futuros se esse quoad obedientiam quam ipsi promittent recipentes ordinem presbyteratus, devovendo se servitio diocesis cum zelo et perseverantia, si non placeat Deo seipsos vocare aliquando ad statum majoris perfectionis."—Nilles, *Selectae Disputationes*, p. 121.

[83] Nilles, *ibid.*, p. 107.

Pontiff. Should a lower superior want to recede from the canonical norms for the admission of candidates to the seminary, he must have recourse to the Holy See. The necessity of such recourse was illustrated in the pontifical constitutions which bestowed on the Cardinal protectors of a German college in Rome the ordinary faculty of bishops in a diocesan seminary.[84] When they thought it advisable that the liberty of clerics to enter religion be somewhat restricted on account of particular circumstances,[85] they did not arrogate to themselves this power, although they had been authorized to approve new laws. But they thought it best to have recourse to the Supreme Pontiff, who insisted on the cleric's liberty to embrace the religious life, but only under certain specified conditions.[86] Yet the Pope did not in any way grant the Cardinal protectors and those in charge of the funds the right to demand any reimbursement from the clerical students entering religion.[87]

It is to be noted that a clear distinction is here made between possible reimbursement to be made by a cleric entering the religious life and that required of a cleric who returns to the lay state after having received a free seminary training. Those belonging to the latter group may be bound by synodal law to restore money spent on them by the seminary. There is nothing against ecclesiastical law or justice in the adoption of statutes aiming at that end, as is seen from the Provincial Synod of Bordeaus (1583), which demanded for every seminarian a bondsman who would be willing to pay the expenses of his seminary training if he did not persevere in the ecclesiastical state;[88] the

[84] Cordara, *Historia Collegii Germanici et Hungarici*, lib. 4, n. 13, as cited by Nilles, *ibid.*, p. 108.

[85] Cordara, *ibid.*, n. 29.

[86] Cordara, *ibid.*, n. 28.

[87] Nilles, *ibid.*, p. 109.

[88] Jean Hardouin, *Conciliorum Collectio Regia Maxima* (12 vols., Parisiis 1715), X, 1383. Great care must be taken by the superiors, however, so as not morally to compel a seminarian to advance to the priesthood for fear that he will be burdened with a considerable debt if he relinquishes his clerical studies.

Provincial Synod of Malines, Belgium (1609);[89] the Provincial Synod of Naples (1699), which required a pledge from the students and their parents that they would make good the expenses of their board, both in case they abandoned the ranks of the clergy and in case they refused an office or duty assigned to them by the bishop;[90] and the III Provincial Council of Cincinnati (1861).[91]

Neither was the approval of the Holy See lacking in legislation which required compensation for the free seminary training upon the cleric's return to the lay state, as is gathered from the case of the synodal statutes in Cesena, Italy,[92] and of that of the Abbey of Nonantola, Italy, which asked the Holy See:

> "An servandae sunt constitutiones synodales, quibus cavetur dandam esse ab alumnis fidejussionem de restituendis alimentis et expensis pro eis factis, casu quo ipsi, propria culpa, ad sacrum presbyteratus ordinem non promoveantur?" to which the Sacred Congregation of the Council, on December 1, 1685, answered: "Affirmative, ita ut pro pauperibus sufficiat obligatio conjunctorum."[93]

[89] Tit. XX, cap. 4, which decreed: "Singuli in sua ad seminarium assumptione declarabunt se habere animum ad statum ecclesiasticum; et insuper promittent, se, cum idonei invenientur, id muneris in ecclesia Dei subituros quod nos ipsis injungemus, aut refusuros expensas, quibus seminarium affecerint."—Claeys Bouuaert, *De Canonica Cleri Saecularis Obedientia,* p. 249, not. 4.

[90] *Collectio Lacensis* (7 vols. bound in 8, Friburgi Brisgoviae, 1870-1892), I, col. 229.

[91] It ruled as follows: "Decreverunt patres exigendam esse ab omnibus alumnis seminariorum, infra sex menses post inceptam philosophiam, seriam promissionem iuxta normam collegiorum pontificorum, eos nempe constitutiones seminarii observaturos, ordines sacros suscepturos, quando superioribus visum fuerit, confectisque studiis, in propria dioecesi ad nutum ordinarii in divinis exercendis perpetuo mansuros. Insuper statuerunt ab iisdem exigendam esse eodem tempore promissionem scriptis exaratam, se proprio ordinario totam pecuniae summam, eorum educatione expensam, restituturos, si qua a suscipiendis ordinibus resilierint."—*Decreta,* n. 5; Mansi, XLVIII, 366; *Collectio Lacensis,* III, col. 225.

[92] *Supra,* p. 151.

[93] Monacelli, *Formularium Legale,* supplement to tom. II, n. 108.

In the light of historical legislation, the solution to the question presented at the beginning of this discussion must be in the negative, i.e., synodal statutes may not licitly demand reimbursement from a cleric who transfers to the religious life after he has received free seminary training and support.[94]

E. The Obligation of Service to the Diocese for a Specified Number of Years

Besides the promise of reverence and obedience in the ordination ceremony and the oath for the canonical title of "service of the diocese," there might be demanded of major clerics in some diocese another promise binding them to the service of the diocese for a minimum number of years, and that to the exclusion of entry into the religious life. Could the violation of this promise be advanced as a basis for alleging the consequence of grave spiritual harm to souls in the diocese? But would an alleged assertion of such harm on account of the violation of the hypothetical promise find canonical approval? Or, more basically, is an authority inferior to the Pope qualified to impose upon his major clerics a promise of this description?

Historical evidences discover for us the mind of the Roman Pontiffs. In 1859, the Bishop of Orleans asked Pope Pius IX for a prohibition against the entry into religion by the secular clerics of his diocese. The same prohibition was to extend over a three-year period after the priests' ordination. The Sacred Congregation of Bishops and Regulars, after a thorough study of the difficult request, submitted its observations to the Holy Father and was commanded to send a negative reply to the local ordinary.[95]

[94] If the local ordinary and the superior of a religious institute have agreed that the religious community will reimburse the diocese for the amount spent on a seminarian's education when the latter seeks admission into the institute, that arrangement can be said to be quite commendable, especially if the diocese does likewise when a seminarian for a religious institute transfers to a seminary for the diocesan clergy.

[95] S. C. Ep. et Reg., *Aurelianen.*, 20 dec. 1859—*Fontes,* n. 1979.

A similar solution was given to a difficulty that had arisen between a certain bishop of Bavaria and four of his deacons. The latter refused to oblige themselves in writing to serve the diocese for at least six years after their ordination to the priesthood. Whereupon a disagreement arose between them and their bishop, and the deacons had recourse to the Holy See. Pope Leo XIII expressed his desire that the clerics be ordained to the priesthood after promising the ordinary reverence and obedience to their bishop and taking the oath of "service of the diocese," for such time as it pleased God not to call them to a state of greater perfection.[96]

An instance of similar importance is the lengthy reply of Pope Benedict XIV to Cardinal Quirini in 1747. The Cardinal had requested the Roman Pontiff to restrict by definite legislation the freedom of secular clerics to enter as members into religious communities. Nevertheless, in his letter the Holy Father did not see fit to enact legislation of this nature. In individual cases wherein grave harm resulted for any particular church, so the Pope maintained, the bishops has sufficient authority to oppose the departure of a cleric from his diocese.[97]

That the cleric entered with his bishop a tacit contract of fulfilling the work of the ecclesiastical ministry at least for a notable period of time by the very fact that he had received gratuitous education is an extreme view taken by at least one author. Furthermore, he held that a cleric is bound by the terms of this tacit contract to the extent that he could not enter the religious life for a determined period of time without the consent of his bishop.[98] However, the present writer does not agree that such a tacit contract is entered into by the fact alone of accepting a gratuitous education. Consequently the future possibility

[96] *Supra*, pp. 151-152.

[97] Ep. *Ex quo*, §18—*Fontes*, n. 374.

[98] Daris, *Quaestiones canonico-civiles de Statu Religioso*, IV, 60, as quoted by McBride, 179.

either of excardination from the diocese or entrance into religion must be admitted.[99]

The conclusion, which is also the answer to the questions asked previously, is that an additional special promise of priestly service to the diocese for a definite number of years, to the exclusion of the possibility of entry into religion during this same period of time, may not be demanded by the local ordinary. Only the Holy See can permit the making of a promise which thus would serve as an impediment against admission into the novitiate.[100]

ARTICLE 5. AN ARRANGEMENT FOR THE PREVENTION OF GRAVE HARM TO SOULS

A. The Necessity of an Attempt to Avoid the Spiritual Injury

If the circumstances in a diocese are of such a nature that a major cleric's departure to enter a religious community gives rise to grave spiritual injury for a number of people, then one of two requisite conditions for constituting this impediment is fulfilled. But the presence of one condition without the other is not sufficient to justify the local ordinary's opposition to the cleric's admission into the novitiate. The other condition that must be satisfied is that the ordinary, after judging that the harm will result from the cleric's departure from the diocese, is not able in one way or another to arrange for the prevention of the grave harm to souls. Only after an endeavor to do this has failed does the impediment take effect. The juridic importance of the second requisite is emphasized by the fact that it was not contained in the original schema of the Code,[101]

[101] In the schema of canonical legislation of 1912, the law read as follows (under canon 414, 1°): "Illicite, sed valide admittuntur: Clerici in sacris constituti, inconsulto loci Ordinario aut eodem contradicente ex eo quod eorum discessus in grave detrimentum cedat."—P. Gasparri, *Schema Codicis Iuris Canonici* (4 vols. bound in 2, Romae: Typis Polyglottis Vaticanis, 1912), I, 211.

[99] Cf. canons 107, 112, 114, 116.

[100] Cf. can. 542, 1°*ult.*

but was added later, so that the impediment now reads:

> Illicite, sed valide admittuntur: Clerici in sacris constituti, inconsulto loci Ordinario aut eodem contradicente ex eo quod eorum discessus in grave detrimentum cedat, *quod aliter vitari minime possit* (italics added).

The import of the italicized phrase, therefore, is that some one has at least an implied obligation to take positive action in order to avoid the threatening harm to souls and to clear the way for the cleric's entrance into religion. Since the greater spiritual welfare of the cleric is here involved, an obligation arising also from charity would seem to require similar attention and planning. But who is better qualified to prevent the grave spiritual harm occasioned, in an individual case, by a major cleric's departure than the local ordinary who has ordinary jurisdiction for making canonical appointments to various positions and offices in his diocese? It is the local ordinary, consequently, upon whom rests the duty of trying to forestall the said injury. If he has some special authority delegated to him by law, through the employment of which power he is able to remedy the situation, he is expected to use that power. For instance, if the local ordinary judges that the injury will result from the fact that many people will be deprived of the opportunity to attend Holy Mass on Sundays, he should make use of his faculty permitting him to allow his priests to binate according to the norm of canon 806, §2. Thus the binated Mass of another priest would offer the same opportunity to the faithful which they previously had from the ministry of the major cleric who now intends to leave the diocese to enter religion. In like manner, if the local ordinary decides that the said harm will arise from the lack of catechetical instruction, he should seek the possible assistance of religious, even the exempt, as a remedy.[102] If, from other sources, he foresees grave spiritual harm arising from the major cleric's absence, he should attempt

[102] Cf. can. 1334.

as best he can to ameliorate the condition so as to free the cleric in his proposal to enter the religious life.

Even after having given serious thought and reflection to the various possible ways of averting the spiritual harm, the local ordinary might be convinced that he cannot find a solution for preventing the said spiritual injury and that the cleric must remain in the service of the diocese. Accordingly he has the right to the continued service of the major cleric in the diocese. And for that period of time during which the conditions of the diocese remain unchanged the cleric is obliged to remain. The delay of the cleric's departure is justified, therefore, for as long as the local ordinary judges that circumstances are the same. Later, when conditions have improved, e.g., through ordinations or perhaps the establishment of a religious house from which additional priestly assistance might be sought for the ministrations of the faithful, the ordinary is no longer justified in his original decision. Whereupon, after such a delay, the cleric should be informed of his freedom to transfer to the religious life if he still has the intention of doing so.

B. Recourse from the Decision of the Local Ordinary and a Dispensation from the Impediment

Ordinarily, of course, the major cleric is expected to abide by the decision of the local ordinary in regard to the presence of grave harm upon his departure from the diocese to embrace the religious life. If on account of obvious reasons the major cleric perceives that the local ordinary advances this one canonically justified reason for refusal as a mere pretext to prevent the cleric from transferring to a religious house, the cleric is not obliged to comply with the insincere opposition. He can licitly be admitted into the novitiate.[103] While in principle it is true that such a pretext would not be sufficient to constitute an

[103] Cf. Larraona, "Commentarium Codicis," *CpRM*, XVII (1936), 246.

impediment, it is equally true that it is difficult if not impossible to be certain of such pretense. Certainly the presumption would always be in favor of the local ordinary, who has a right to the respect, reverence and obedience of his clerics. Undoubtedly it is he who has the more complete view of the spiritual necessities of the faithful and of his diocese in contradistinction to the cleric whose view of the same needs can easily be narrow and defective.

However, in cases of serious doubt as to the correctness of the local ordinary's judgment, there is permitted a recourse to the Holy See.[104] During the intervening time the cleric is bound by the decision of the ordinary. For the receiving of this recourse, the Sacred Congregation of Religious is considered competent by reason of the subject, i.e., a possible candidate to the religious life, and also by reason of the subject matter, i.e., the religious life itself. Furthermore, because of the fact that the good of the diocese is concerned, the same competency is enjoyed by the Sacred Congregation of the Council.[105]

If a major cleric is bound by the impediment against licit entrance into religion either on account of the lack of consultation or on account of the justified opposition of the local ordinary, he may for good reasons seek a dispensation from the impediment from the Sacred Congregation of Religious.[106] According to Schaefer, the Sacred Congregation is accustomed to ask the local ordinary not to impede a cleric's entrance into religion if it is discovered that the ordinary is not canonically justified in his opposition to the cleric.[107]

[104] Sylvius Romani, *Institutiones Juris Canonici*, Vol. I (Romae: Via Machiavelli, 50, 1941), p. 363, n. 699.

[105] Schaefer, *De Religiosis*, p. 440, n. 803; cf. Larraona, *ibid.*, pp. 245-246.

[106] Possibly, too, the Sacred Congregation of the Council would grant the dispensation because of the close connection of the implications of this impediment with diocesan administration. Cf. Larraona, *ibid.*, p. 246; Vermeersch-Creusen, *Epitome*, I, n. 680, p. 488.

[107] *De Religiosis*, p. 441, n. 803; cf. Larraona, *ibid.*, p. 246.

A summary of this chapter indicates that a major cleric labors under an impediment against licit admission into the novitiate in the event that: a) the local ordinary objects to his permanent departure from the diocese for the reason that a number of people will suffer serious spiritual harm as a result of the cleric's transfer to a religious institute, and b) if at the same time the said injury cannot be averted by another arrangement undertaken especially by the local ordinary. This impediment does not bind the cleric pereptually, but only for that period of time during which his services are needed to forestall the grave injury to souls. The objection of the local ordinary for any reason other than the one just mentioned finds no justification in the prescriptions of this impediment, and therefore does not bind the cleric. In matters of doubt as to the correctness of the local ordinary's decision and therefore the consequent legality of his opposition, the cleric is obliged to render his obedience. In the meantime, however, he may have recourse to the Sacred Congregation of Religious or the Sacred Congregation of the Council.

CONCLUSIONS

1. The formal impediment against licit admission into the novitiate as outlined in canon 542, 2° *pr*,, is entirely new in the present legislation of the Church. Before the promulgation of the Code clerics were not forbidden under any circumstances to enter the novitiate of a congregation or an order. However, their revocation to a former church was allowed if by their departure serious harm was caused to that church.

2. Minor clerics are not affected by the restrictions of this impediment against the traditional liberty of clerics to embrace the religious life. Much less does the impediment apply to seminarians who have not yet received tonsure. Students from either class of these clerical aspirants may licitly be admitted into the novitiate for the simple reason that they are not influenced by the provisions of canon 542, 2° *pr*.

3. Subdeacons, deacons, priests and prelates in rank inferior to that of bishops come under the restrictions of the impediment. They are the clerics established in major orders referred to in the legislation itself. Whether the impediment is equally applicable to major clerics reduced to the lay state is considered a *dubium iuris*. Hence is practice such clerics are not bound.

4. The local ordinary referred to in canon 542, 2° *pr*., is any one of those mentioned in canon 198. The proper local ordinary of the cleric is the one to be consulted previous to entrance into the religious life. Lack of such consultation produces the impediment against the cleric's licit admission into the novitiate.

5. By the term "consultation" a wider significance is to be understood than a mere notification sent to the local ordinary. The latter may freely express his opinion and observations on the matter at a time and place reasonably convenient to himself. Yet a total lack of any

response to a cleric's expression of intention to enter the religious life may be interpreted as an implict indication that the local ordinary has nothing to offer in the matter of consultation. Moreover, if the local ordinary does express his views and observation the cleric is not thereby placed under any obligation to abide by them, except as indicated in the following paragraph.

6. Only upon the simultaneous fulfillment of these two conditions does the impediment take effect: a) the local ordinary objects to the cleric's permanent departure from the diocese for the reason that a number of people will suffer serious spiritual harm as a result of the cleric's transfer to the religious institute; and b) the said injury cannot be averted by any other provisional arrangement to be attempted especially by the local ordinary. This impediment does not bind perpetually, but only for that period of time during which the cleric's services are needed as a means for forestalling the grave injury impending for souls.

7. The opposition by the local ordinary for any reason other than the fact that souls will suffer a serious injury which cannot otherwise be prevented finds no canonical justification for the detention of a cleric for continued service in the diocese. Hence a cleric thus opposed may licitly be admitted into the novitiate, provided of course that he has previously consulted his local ordinary. Accordingly, in themselves such reasons as a scarcity of priests in a diocese or a gratuitous education extended a cleric in the seminary are not justified motives for the prohibition of a cleric's entry into religion. Only in so far as grave harm will result to souls from such circumstances will reasons of this kind find canonical justification.

8. If in doubt as to the local ordinary's correct decision as to the ensuing grave damage to souls, the cleric is obliged to comply with the judgment of the ordinary. In the meantime, however, he may have recourse to the Sacred Congregation of Religious or to the Sacred Congregation of the Council.

BIBLIOGRAPHY

Sources

Acta Apostolicae Sedis, Commentarium Officiale, Romae, 1909—.

Acta et Decreta Concilii Plenarii Baltimorensis Tertii, A. D. MDCCCLXXXIV, Baltimorae: John Murphy, 1886.

Bruns, H. Th., *Canones Apostolorum et Conciliorum Saeculorum IV, V, VI, VII,* 2 vols., Berolini, 1839.

Bullarum Diplomatum et Privilegiorum Sanctorum Romanorum Pontificum Taurinensis Editio, 24 tomes in 25 vols., Augustae Taurinorum-Neapoli, 1857-1872.

Canones et Decreta Concilii Tridentini, ex ed. Romana 1834 repetiti, Neapoli, 1859.

Codex Iuris Canonici Pii X Pontificis Maximi iussu digestus Benedicti Papae XV auctoritate promulgatus, Romae: Typis Polyglottis Vaticanis, 1917.

Codex Regularum Monasticarum et Canonicarum, collected by Saint Benedict of Aniane, 6 vols., Augustae Vindelicorum, 1759.

Codicis Iuris Canonici Fontes cura Emi Petri Card. Gasparri editi, 9 vols., Romae (postea Civitate Vaticana): Typis Polyglottis Vaticanis, 1923-1939 (Vols. VII, VIII, IX ed. cura et studio Emi Iustiniani Card. Serédi).

Collectanea S. Congregationis de Propaganda Fide, 2 vols., Romae: Typographia Polyglotta S. C. de Propaganda Fide, 1907.

Collectio Lacensis, 7 vols. bound in 8, Friburgi Brisgoviae, 1870-1892.

Concilii Plenarii Baltimorensis II, in Ecclesia Metropolitana, a die VII. ad diem XXI. Octobris, A. D., MDCCCLXVI., Habiti, et a Sede Apostolica Recogniti, Acta et Decreta, Baltimorae, John Murphy, 1868.

Corpus Iuris Canonici, ed. 2. curavit Aemilius Friedberg, 2 vols., Lipsiae, 1879-1881.

Decretum Gratiani Emendatum et Observationibus Illustratum una cum Glossis, Gregorii XIII Pont. Max. iussu editum, 2 vols., Romae, 1582.

Decretales D. Gregorii IX una cum Glossis Restitutae, Romae, 1582.

Hardouin, Jean, *Conciliorum Collectio Regia Maxima,* 12 vols., Parisiis, 1715.

Holy Bible, The, Translated from the Latin Vulgate, published with the *imprimatur* and approbation of His Eminence Patrick Cardinal Hayes, New York: C. Wilderman, Inc., 1938.

Jaffé, Philippus, *Regesta Pontificum Romanorum ab condita Ecclesia ad annum post Christum natum MCXCVIII,* 2. ed. correctam et auctam auspiciis Gulielmi Wattenbach curaverunt F. Kaltenbrunner, S. Loewenfeld, P. Ewald, 2 vols., Lipsiae, 1885-1898.

Juris Pontificii de Propaganda Fide Complectens Decreta Instructiones Encyclicas Literas Etc., ed. Raphaelis de Martinis, 7 vols., Romae, 1888-1898.

Liber Sextus Decretalium D. Bonifacii Papae VIII suae integritati una cum Clementinis et Extravagantibus earumque Glossis restitutis, Romae, 1582.

Mansi, Joannes Dominicus, *Sacrorum Conciliorum Nova et Amplissima Collectio*, 53 vols. in 60, Paris-Arnhem-Leipzig, 1901-1927.

Monumenta Germaniae Historica, Epistolae, tom. I, II, ed. P. Ewald et L. M. Hartman, Berolini, 1887-1899.

———, *Leges Sectio II, Capitularia Regum Francorum*, tom. I, ed. A. Boretius, Hannoveriae, 1883.

Nicene and Post Nicene Fathers, 2. series, 14 vol., New York: Parker and Company, 1890-1900.

Pontificale Romanum, 3 parts in 1 vol., Mechliniae: H. Dessain, 1895.

Potthast, A., *Regesta Pontificum Romanorum inde ab anno post Christum Natum 1198 ad Annum 1304*, 2 vols., Berolini, 1874-1875.

Regula Sancti Pachomii, in Migne, *Patrologiae Cursus Completus, Series Latina*, XXIII, 70.

Regula Sanctorum Serapionis, Macarii, Paphnutii et alterius Macarii, in *Codex Regularum Monasticarum et Canonicarum*, by Saint Benedict of Aniane, Vol. I.

Sancti Benedicti Regula Monachorum, ed. by C. Butler, Friburgi Brisgoviae, 1912.

Schroeder, H. J., *Canons and Decrees of the Council of Trent*, St. Louis, Mo.: Herder, 1941.

Reference Works

Alphonsus Liguori, St., *Theologia Moralis*, ed. novissima, 6 vols., Parisiis, (no date).

Antoninus, St., *Summa Theologica in Quattuor Partes distributa*, Veronae, 1740.

Andrews, E. A., *Latin-English Lexicon*, New York: Harper Brothers, 1870.

Augustine, Charles, *A Commentary on the New Code of Canon Law*, Vol. II, 4. ed., St. Louis: Herder, 1923.

Azorius, Ioannes, *Institutiones Morales*, 3 vols., Brixiae, 1617.

Berutti, Christophorus, *Institutiones Iuris Canonici*, Vol. II, Pars I (1943), Vol. III (1936), Taurini-Romae: Marietti.

Beste, Udalricus, *Introductio in Codicem*, 3. ed., Collegeville: St. John's Abbey Press, 1946.

Blat, Albertus, *Commentarium Textus Codicis Iuris Canonici*, 6 vols., 1919-1927, and Lib. II, Pars 2-3, 3. ed., 1938, Romae.

Bouix, Dominicus, *Tractatus de Jure Regularium*, 2 vols., Parisiis, 1857.

Bouscaren, Lincoln, and Ellis, Adam, *Canon Law, A Text and Commentary*, Milwaukee: Bruce, copyright, 1946.

Brown, James, *Non-Age, Fear, Fraud, Crime, and Oath "ex Instituto Sanctae Sedis," as Diriment Impediments to Entrance into the Novitiate*, The Catholic University of America Canon Law Studies, Unpublished Licentiate Thesis, Washington, D. C.: The Catholic University of America, 1949.

Cappello, Felix, *Summa Iuris Canonici*, 3 vols., Vols. I-II, 4. ed., Vol. III, 3. ed., Romae: apud Aedes Universitatis Gregorianae, 1945-1948.

———, *Tractatus Canonico-Moralis de Sacramentis*, Vol. IV, 2. ed., Augustae Taurinorum, Romae, 1947.

Chelodi, Ioannes, *Ius Canonicum de Personis*, 3. ed., Trento, 1942.

———, *Ius de Personis iuxta Codicem Iuris Canonici*, 2. ed., Tridenti: Libr. Edit. Tridentum, 1927.

———, *Ius Poenale et Ordo Procedendi in Iudiciis Criminalibus iuxta Codicem Iuris Canonici*, 4. ed., recognita et aucta a Vigilio Dalpiaz, Tridenti: Ardesi, 1935.

Cicognani, Amleto Giovanni, *Canon Law*, 2. ed., Westminster, Maryland: The Newman Bookshop, 1935.

Claeys Bouuaert, F., and Simenon, G., *Manuale Juris Canonici*, Vol. I, 5. ed., Gandae et Leodii: apud Auctores, 1939.

Claeys Bouuaert, F., *De Canonica Cleri Saecularis Obedientia*, Lovanii, 1904.

Cocchi, Guidus, *Commentarium in Codicem Iuris Canonici*, Vol. IV, 3. ed., Taurinorum Augustae, 1932.

Cordara, Julius, *Historia Collegii Germanici et Hungarici*, Romae, 1770.

Coronata, Matthaeus Conte A., *Institutiones Iuris Canonici*, Vol. I, 2. ed., Taurini: Marietti, 1939.

Daris, Joseph, *Quaestiones canonico-civiles de Statu Religioso, Praelectiones canonicae*, 5 vols., Leodii: Verhoven—Debeur, 1863-1874.

Delatte, Paul, *A Commentary on the Rule of St. Benedict*, translated by Dom Justin McCann, New York: Benziger Brothers, 1921.

De Meester, A., *Juris Canonici et Juris Canonico-civilis Compendium*, 3 vols. in 4, nova ed., Brugis, 1921-1928.

Dukehart, Claude, *State of Perfection and the Secular Priest*, The Catholic University of America Studies in Sacred Theology, 2. series, n. 46, Washington, D. C.: The Catholic University of America Press, 1949, microcarded 1950.

Fagnanus, Prosper, *Commentaria In Quinque Libros Decretalium*, 5 vols. in 3, Venetiis, 1709.

Fanfani, Ludovicus, *De Iure Religiosorum ad Normam Codicis Iuris Canonici*, 2. ed., Taurini-Romae: Marietti, 1925.

Ferraris, Lucius, *Prompta Bibliotheca Canonica, Juridica, Moralis, Theologica, necnon Ascetica, Polemica, Rubricistica, Historica,* ed. novissima, 9 vols., Romae, 1885-1899.

Findlay, Stephen W., *Canonical Norms Governing the Deposition and Degradation of Clerics,* The Catholic University of America Canon Law Studies, n. 130, Washington, D. C.: The Catholic University of America Press, 1941.

Gasparri, P., *Schema Codicis Iuris Canonici,* 4 vols. bound in 2, Romae: Typis Polyglottis Vaticanis, 1912.

———, *Tractatus Canonicus de sacra ordinatione,* 2 vols., Parisiis: Delhomme et Briguet, 1893.

Goyeneche, S., *Iuris Canonici Summa Principia,* Vol. I, Romae: Typis Polyglottis, 1935.

Guido de Bayso, *Rosarium seu in Decretorum Volumen Commentaria,* Venetiis, 1577.

Hallier, Franciscus, *De sacris electionibus et ordinationibus,* 2. ed., 3 vols., Romae, 1740.

Hostiensis (Henricus de Segusio), *Commentaria in Quinque Libros Decretalium,* 5 vols. in 3, Venetiis, 1581.

Innocentius IV (Sinibalso de'Fieschi), *Apparatus super Quinque Libris Decretalium,* Strassburg, 1478.

Joannes Andreae, *In Sex Decretalium Libros Novella Commentaria,* 6 vols. in 5, Venetiis, 1581.

Köstler, Rudolf, *Wörterbuch zum Codex Iuris Canonici,* München: Verlag Joseph Kösel & Friedrich Pustet, 1927-1929.

Lucidi, Angelus, *De Visitatione Sacrorum Liminum,* 3. ed., 3 vols., Romae, 1883.

McBride, James T., *Incardination and Excardination of Seculars,* The Catholic University of America Canon Law Studies, n. 145, Washington, D. C.: The Catholic University of America Press, 1941.

Migne, J. P., *Patrologiae Cursus Completus, Series Latina,* 221 vols., 1844-1864.

———, *Patrologiae Cursus Completus, Series Graeca,* 161 vols. in 164, Parisiis, 1856-1866.

Monacelli, Franciscus, Formularium Legale Practicum, 3 vols., Venetiis, 1736-1751.

Maroto, Philippus, *Institutiones Iuris Canonici,* Vol. I, 3. ed., Romae: apud *Commentarium pro Religiosis,* 1921.

Nilles, Nicolaus, *Selectae Disputationes Academicae Juris Ecclesiastici,* Oeniponte, 1886.

Noldin, H., and Schmitt, A., *Summa Theologiae Moralis,* 27. ed., 3 vols., New York: Frederick Pustet, 1940-1941.

Oesterle, Gerardus, *Praelectiones Iuris Canonici,* Vol. I, Romae: Collegio S. Anselmi, 1931.

Panormitanus, Abbas (Nicolaus de Tudeschis), *Commentaria in Quinque Libros Decretalium*, 5 vols. in 7, Venetiis, 1578.

Passerinus, Petrus, *Inspectiones Morales de Statibus Hominum*, 3 vols., Lucae, 1732.

Piatus Montensis, *Praelectiones Iuris Regularis*, 3. ed., 2 vols., Parisiis, *imprimatur* 1906.

Prümmer, Dominicus, *Manuale Iuris Canonici*, 3. ed., 2 vols., Friburgi Brisgoviae, 1922.

Regatillo, Eduardus, *Institutiones Iuris Canonici*, Vol. 1, 3. ed., Santander: Sal Terrae, 1948.

Romani, Sylvius, *Institutiones Juris Canonici*, Vol. I, Romae: Via Machiavelli, 50, 1941.

Rufinus, *Die Summa Decretorum des Magister Rufinus*, Paderborn, 1902.

Sanchez, Thomas, *Opus Morale in Praecepta Decalogi*, 2 vols., Lugduni, 1661.

Sancti Thomae Aquinatis, *Opera Omnia, cum commentariis Thomae de Vio Caietani*, Tom. X, Romae, 1899.

Schaefer, Timotheus, *De Religiosis Ad Normam Codicis Iuris Canonici*, 4. ed., Typis Polyglottis Vaticanis: Roma, 1947.

Schmalzgrueber, Franciscus, *Jus Ecclesiasticum Universum*, 5 vols. in 12, Romae, 1843-1845.

Schmier, Franciscus, *Jurisprudentia Canonico-Civilis*, 2 vols., Venetiis, 1754.

Schroll, Sister M. Alfred, *Benedictine Monasticism*, New York: Columbia University Press, 1941.

Schultz, F., *Latin Grammar*, 36. ed., Frederick Pustet Co., Inc.: New York, no date.

Suarez, Franciscus, *Opera Omnia*, 28 vols., Parisiis, 1856-1861.

Sweeney, Francis P., *The Reduction of Clerics to the Lay State*, The Catholic University of America Canon Law Studies, n. 223, Washington, D. C.: The Catholic University of America Press, 1945.

Sylvius, Franciscus, *Commentarium in Summam Sancti Thomae*, 3. ed., 6 vols., Antverpiae, 1667.

Tamburinius, A., de Marradio, *De Iure Abbatum et Aliorum Praelatorum*, 3 vols., Lugduni, 1640.

Thomas Aquinas, St., *Summa Theologica*, English translation by the Fathers of the English Dominican Province, 3 vols., Benziger Brothers, Inc., 1948.

Thomassinus, Ludovicus, *Vetus et Nova Ecclesiae Disciplina circa Beneficia et Beneficiarios*, ed. postrema, 3 vols., Magontiaci, 1691.

Toso, Albertus, *Ad Codicem Iuris Canonici Benedicti XV Pont. Max.*

Auctoritate Promulgatum Commentaria Minora, 5 vols., Romae: Jus Pontificium, 1920-1927.

Vermersch, Arthurus, *De Religiosis Institutis et Personis*, 2 vols., Brugis: sumptibus Beyaert, 1902.

Vermeersch, A., and Creusen, I., *Epitome Iuris Canonici*, Vol. I, 7. ed., Mechliniae: Romae, H. Dessain, 1949.

Wernz, Franciscus, *Ius Decretalium*, 2. ed., Vol. III, Romae, 1908; 3. ed., Vol. II, Prati, 1915.

Wernz, Franciscus, and Vidal, Petrus, *Ius Canonicum*, 7 vols. in 8, Romae: Universitas Gregoriana, 1923-1938 (3. ed., Vols. II, 1943, V, 1946; 2. ed., Vol. VI, 1949).

Woywod, Stanislaus, *A Practical Commentary on the Code*, revised and enlarged ed., 2 vols., New York: Joseph F. Wagner, Inc., 1948.

Anonymous, *Praelectiones Juris Canonici habitae in seminario Sancti Sulpitii*, 6. ed., 3 vols. Parisiis, 1886.

Articles

Arendt, G., "De Can. 542 et 981"—*Jus Pontificium*, IV (1924), 184.

Kuttner, Stephan-Smalley, Beryl, "The Glossa Ordinaria to the Gregorian Decretals"—*The English Historical Review*, LX (1945), 97-105.

Larraona, Arcadius, "Commentarium Codicis"—*CpRM*, XVII (1936), 242-246.

Peinador, A., "Sacerdotium Saeculare et Status Religiosus..."—*CpRM*, XIX (1938), 269-284; XX (1939), 38-49; 313-327.

Woywod, S., "Seminarians Entering Religious Community and Compensation to Diocese for Expenses Incurred"—*The Homiletic and Pastoral Review*, XXIX (1929), 996-998.

Anonymous, "De Clericorum Ingressu in Religionem"—*Periodica de Re Canonica et Morali utilia praesertim Religiosis et Missionariis*, XIII (1924-1925), 145-151; 213-215.

Anonymous, "De Can. 542"—*Il Monitore Ecclesiastico*, Serie IV, Vol. V, Fasc. X (Ottobre 1924), 311 sq.; fasc. XII (Dicembre 1924), 367-368.

Periodicals

Commentarium pro Religiosis (later [1935] *Commentarium pro Religiosis et Missionariis*), Romae, 1920—

Il Monitore Ecclesiastico, Romae, 1876-1948.

Jus Pontificium, Romae, 1921-1940.

Periodica de Religiosis et Missionariis, Brugis, 1905-1919; from 1920: *Periodica de Re Canonica et Morali utilia praesertim Religiosis et Missionariis*, Brugis, 1920-1927; from 1927: *Periodica de Re*

Morali, Canonica, Liturgica, Brugis (1927-1936) et Romae (1937—).
The English Historical Review, London, 1886—
The Homiletic and Pastoral Review, New York, 1900—

Abbreviations

AAS—*Acta Apostolicae Sedis.*
Bruns—*Canones Apostolorum et Conciliorum saec. IV-VII,* ed. Bruns.
C.—*Causa.*
Collectanea S. C. P. F.—*Collectanea Sacrae Congregationis de Propaganda Fide.*
Conc. Trid.—Concilium Tridentinum.
CpRM—*Commentarium pro Religiosis et Missionariis.*
D.—*Distinctio.*
Ep.—*Epistola.*
Fontes—*Codicis Iuris Canonici Fontes cura . . . Gasparri editi.*
JE—Jaffé, *Regesta Pontificum Romanorum* (edited by P. Ewald: from 590-882).
JK—Jaffé, *op. cit.* (edited by F. Kaltenbrunner: to the year 590).
JL—Jaffé, *op. cit.* (edited by S. Loewenfeld: from 882-1198).
Ibid.—*Ibidem* (the preceding reference).
Instr.—*Instructio.*
Loc. cit.—*Loco citato.*
Mansi—Mansi, J. D., *Sacrorum Conciliorum Nova et Amplissima Collectio.*
MPL—(Migne, *Patrologia Latina*) Migne, Jacques Paul, *Patrologiae Cursus Completus—Series Latina.*
Op. cit.—*Opere citato.*
R. J.—*Regula Juris.*
S. C. C.—Sacra Congregatio Concilii.
S. C. Consist.—Sacra Congregatio Consistorialis.
S. C. Ep. et Reg.—Sacra Congregatio Episcoporum et Regularium.
S. C. Sacr.—Sacra Congregatio de Sacramentis.

BIOGRAPHICAL NOTE

Leo Koesler was born on March 24, 1921, in Lindsay, Texas. After receiving his elementary education in Saint Peter's Parochial School, he attended high school and college at Subiaco College-Academy, Subiaco, Arkansas, where he received the degree of Bachelor of Arts on May 27, 1943. He entered the novitate at New Subiaco Abbey, Subiaco, Arkansas on September 13, 1940, pronounced temporary vows on September 14, 1941, and solemn vows on September 14, 1944. He was ordained to the priesthood at Saint Andrew's Cathedral, Little Rock, Arkansas, on June 15, 1946. In the fall of 1948 he was sent to the Catholic University of America in Washington, D. C., to pursue a graduate course of studies in the School of Canon Law. The Baccalaureate in Canon Law was received from the Catholic University of America in June, 1949, and the Licentiate in Canon Law, in June, 1950.

CANON LAW STUDIES*

327. Koesler, Rev. Leo, O.S.B., J.C.L., Entrance into the Novitiate by Clerics in Major Orders.
328. McFarland, Rev. Norman E., J.C.L., Religious Vocation—Its Juridic Concept.
329. Wiest, Rev. Donald Herman, O.F.M., Cap., S.T.D., J.C.L., The Precensorship of Books.
330. De Witt, Rev. Max George, A.B., J.C.L., The Cessation of Delegated Power.
331. Mathis, Rev. Marcian John, O.F.M., J.C.L., The Constitution and Supreme Administration of Regional Seminaries Subject to the Sacred Congregation for the Propagation of the Faith in China.
332. Schorr, Rev. George F., A.B., J.C.L., The Law of the Celebret.
333. Sheehy, Rev. Robert Francis, A.B., J.C.L., The Sacred Congregation of the Sacraments: Its Competence in the Roman Curia.
334. Shields, Rev. Joseph A., A.B., J.C.L., Deprivation of the Clerical Garb.
335. Uricheck, Rev. George Edward, A.B., J.C.L., De forma celebrationis matrimonii in Ecclesiis Orientalibus ante Motu Proprio *Crebrae Allatae* et post.
336. De Pauw, Rev. Gommar Albert Leo Julian Maria, J.C.L., The Legal Status of Catholic Elementary Schools in Belgium, 1830-1950.

---

* For a complete list of the available numbers of this series apply to the Catholic University of America Press, 620 Michigan Avenue, N. E., Washington 17, D. C.

ALPHABETICAL INDEX

www.ingramcontent.com/pod-product-compliance
Lightning Source LLC
LaVergne TN
LVHW050232080826
844660LV00012B/520

* 9 7 8 0 8 1 3 2 2 4 9 8 5 *